INCLUSIVE HYMNS FOR
LIBERATING CHRISTIANS

Jann Aldredge-Clanton
with composer Larry E. Schultz

EAKIN PRESS ◆ Fort Worth, Texas

Copyright © 2006
By Jann Aldredge-Clanton & Larry E. Schultz
Published By Eakin Press
An Imprint of Wild Horse Media Group
P.O. Box 331779
Fort Worth, Texas 76163
1-817-344-7036
www.EakinPress.com
ALL RIGHTS RESERVED
1 2 3 4 5 6 7 8 9
Paperback ISBN 978-1-68179-302-3
Hardback ISBN 978-1-68179-286-6
eBook ISBN 978-1-68179-285-9

CONTENTS

Introduction 9

JUSTICE AND PEACEMAKING

1. Sister Spirit, Brother Spirit
2. Come Now, O Wisdom
3. Let Justice Roll Like Flowing Streams
4. God Like a Woman Long in Labor Cries
5. Rise Up, All People
6. Our Mother-Father God, We Praise Your Prophets Bold
7. O Great Creator, Loving Friend
8. O Brother-Sister Spirit, Come
9. O Mother-Father of Us All
10. Let Justice Like Waters Roll Down
11. Gather Us Under Your Warm Wings
12. O Come, Join Hands, All Violence Cease
13. How Long, Christ-Sophia?
14. Great Wisdom, Queen of All
15. Join Now with New Power, Marching on for Peace
16. Wake Us All, O Christ-Sophia
17. Come, All Who Long for Peace and Justice on the Earth

PARTNERSHIP AND VOCATION

18. O Spirit of Power
19. Welcome Our Sister-Brother Creator
20. Great Friend of All People
21. Sister-Brother Spirit, Come
22. Our God Is a Mother and a Father
23. Through Distant Lands and Over Stormy Seas
24. Rise and Speak Out

25. God Is She and He Together
26. Holy Christ-Sophia
27. O Christ-Sophia, Holy One
28. Awake to the Voice of Wisdom

LIBERATION

29. Creative Spirit, Strong and Kind
30. Hark! Wisdom's Urgent Cry
31. Come, Father-Mother, Friend and Guide
32. Come, Sisters, Brothers, Come
33. Friend and Source of All Creation
34. O Christ-Sophia, Give Us Power
35. Stir Us Out of Our Safe Nest, Mother Eagle
36. Out of the Depths Christ-Sophia Is Calling
37. Tread Lightly on Your Heavy Path
38. Our Mother-Father God Is Near
39. Christ-Sophia, Wise and Fair
40. God Walks with Us

RESURRECTION AND ABUNDANT LIFE

41. O Holy Spirit, Mystery Within
42. Listen, Now We Tell a Mystery
43. O Wisdom in Our Hearts
44. Love Rises Up
45. Come, Sister-Brother Spirit
46. El Shaddai, O Holy One
47. Father-Mother, Kind and Loving
48. Womb of All Creation Flowing
49. Rise Up, O People, Proclaim Christ-Sophia Has Risen
50. Our God Will Carry Us
51. O Christ-Sophia, Rise

NEW CREATION

52. Celebrate a New Day Dawning
53. Like a Mother with Her Children
54. Creative Spirit, Come

55. Loving Friend, Who Walks Beside Us
56. Be Still and Know
57. Welcome New Wineskins
58. Creator God of Many Names
59. Christ-Sophia, Well of Freedom

COMFORT AND HEALING

60. Come, Weak and Weary Ones
61. Are You Good and Are You Strong?
62. God Like a Mother Comes Tenderly Near
63. Our Mother-Father Cares
64. O Sister-Brother Spirit, Rise
65. God Like a Mother Hen
66. Our God Like a Mother Will Come
67. With Arms of Comfort God Comes Near
68. Come, Christ-Sophia, Healing Power
69. Share Our Grief, O Christ-Sophia
70. Come to Me, All You with Heavy Hearts
71. Hear Our Prayer, O Christ-Sophia

CELEBRATION AND PRAISE

72. We Praise Our God of Many Names
73. A Living Celebration of Christ's Love
74. O Mother-Father God
75. O Great Creator
76. Praise Ruah, Spirit Who Gives Birth
77. Come, Holy Beauty
78. The Heavens Sing the Majesty of All That Ruah Made
79. Let All the Creation Sing Forth with Elation
80. Our Strong and Tender God We Praise
81. New Miracles Unfold
82. Praise Our God, Eternal Goodness

MINISTRY AND MISSION

83. O Sister-Brother Spirit
84. Our Mother Within Us

85. Hope of Glory, Living in Us
86. Send Us Forth, O Christ-Sophia
87. We Claim Your Support, Christ-Sophia, Our Rock
88. Come, Christ-Sophia, Our Way
89. Rise Up, O Christ-Sophia
90. O Flower Blooming, Deep in Pain
91. Go Forth, O Christ-Sophia

THE CHURCH YEAR

Advent

92. Midwife Divine Now Calls Us
93. O Come, Christ-Sophia
94. Sophia, Wisdom Deep in Our Souls

Christmas

95. Christ-Sophia Now We Welcome
96. Christ-Sophia Now We Praise
97. O Christ-Sophia, Be Born in Us
98. Sound Forth the News That Wisdom Comes

Epiphany

99. O Holy Darkness, Loving Womb
100. What Wondrous Thing

Lent

101. If This Is the Fast
102. O Mother Rock Who Bore Us
103. Do You Want to Be Healed?

Palm Sunday

104. O Blessed Christ-Sophia

Easter

105. Christ-Sophia Lives Today
106. Up from the Grave

Pentecost
107. O Holy Spirit, Come Dwell in Our Souls
108. Come, Holy Spirit, to Change Us
109. We Gather with Hope and a Vision of Peace

OTHER SPECIAL OCCASIONS

Communion
110. Come and Feast, for All Are Welcomed
111. We Invite All to Join Our Circle Wide

Ordinations
112. Come, Thou from Whom All Blessings Flow

Weddings/Unions
113. Arise, My Love

Thanksgiving
114. Christ-Sophia Now We Bless

Earth Day
115. We Give Thanks to You, Dear Earth

Independence Day
116. We Sound a Call to Freedom

Notes. 145

Topical Index of Hymns 151

Index of Scripture References. 179

Index of Composers, Authors, and Sources 183

Alphabetical Index of Tunes 185

Metrical Index of Tunes. 189

First Lines and Titles Index. 193

INTRODUCTION

The words we sing in worship matter. Words carry great power. Words spoken in worship carry greater power because of the sacred value given to them. Words sung in worship carry the greatest power to shape belief and action. The music embeds words in the memory of singers. I can recite from memory all stanzas of most of the songs in the hymnal I grew up with in church. But I have little recall of the sermons, even though my father was the preacher.

In the twenty-first century, faith communities struggle to proclaim Good News in a dramatically changing world. Many traditional hymn texts contain archaic language and theology. Some even inadvertently support injustice and exclusivity. Congregations are seeking hymns that more nearly reflect their beliefs. The hymns in this collection focus on the Gospel of liberation, justice, and abundant life for everyone.

The lyrics of these hymns draw from the prophetic, liberating tradition in Scripture. I have based the hymns on biblical texts and include the references with the hymns. Biblical themes, phrases, and images form the foundation for all the hymns. Predominant themes are peace, justice, resurrection, abundant life, liberation, new creation, and partnership in relationships.

The music of hymns touches my earliest memories and resonates in my soul. My first feelings of awe came with the music of congregation and organ joined in praise to the Creator. Among the first pieces of music I learned to play on the piano were hymns. On family vacations we sang hymns to make the miles pass by more quickly. On one long trip I won a family hymn-quoting contest. I loved to hear my father's deep baritone voice singing "There is a Balm in Gilead." My favorite part of worship was always the "song service."

When I first became aware of the importance of inclusive language in hymns, I began trying to change words as I sang along with the congregation. But this practice brought me disapproving stares and feelings of futility as my lone voice was drowned out by hundreds. When I started advocating in my congregation for changing the exclusive words in these traditional hymns, I heard cries that I was "tampering with the original texts." Gradually I accepted my call to write new lyrics to the traditional hymn tunes I love.

Enthusiastic, grateful responses to my first hymns convinced me that many other people longed for new words to familiar music. So I kept writing hymn texts, more than I had ever imagined. And communities sang them more joyfully than I had ever anticipated. I experienced the power of hymns to liberate, to heal, and to create new life.

Most of the tunes in this collection are traditional hymn tunes. The familiar tunes and biblical imagery in this collection of hymns root participants, while the inclusivity and diversity of the lyrics invite us beyond the divisions, prejudice, and narrowness that have plagued churches and society. These hymns grew in the space between my memory of numinous experiences with music in worship and my imagination of a world of freedom, justice, and peace.

Some of the hymn tunes and texts in this collection are by Larry E. Schultz, who co-authored with me *Imagine God! A Children's Musical Exploring and Expressing Images of God* (Garland, Texas: Choristers Guild, 2004). All of the hymns in this collection come to you with the hope that the music and the words will stir your imagination to soar to new lands and your actions to justice and peacemaking. These hymns also come to you with an invitation to join the adventure of creating and singing new songs.

Variety of Divine Names to Convey the Vastness of our Creator

Our Milky Way Galaxy contains approximately 400 billion stars. The Milky Way is only one of more than a hundred billion galaxies in the universe. Every human being has about ten thousand trillion cells, and DNA that if spliced into a single strand would stretch from Miami to Los Angeles and back 2,270 times. Why would we ever try to limit the Creator of so vast a universe and such complex human beings? Even in this twenty-first century the majority of churches still limit divinity to a small set of masculine names and images, such as "Father," "King," and "Son." At the beginning of a new millennium, most churches still try to cram the great Creator of the universe into a small box.

Divine Mystery exceeds all our thoughts and words. We can never fully express this Mystery. All our language for divinity must then be metaphorical. The infinite Creator of the universe cannot be captured in a few masculine metaphors. Drawing from biblical revelation, these hymns include a wide variety of divine names and images in an attempt to suggest the vastness and all-inclusiveness of our Creator.

The hymn texts in this collection balance masculine and feminine names for deity to expand our vision of the One in whose image we are all created. They pair Father with Mother, Brother with Sister, He with She, Christ with *Sophia* (New Testament Greek word for "Wisdom"). In one of the hymns are these lines: "Sister

Spirit gives us power; Brother Spirit ends all strife. She and He together lead us to a spring of flowing life." Another begins with these lines: "Father-Mother, kind and loving, your abundance we're discovering. You provide and gently nourish; through your grace we fully flourish."

Divine Mystery comes in many forms and feelings. It may be the hope that sings in our souls even in the midst of fear and loss and pain. The hymn "Hope of Glory Living in Us" describes the struggle of blazing new trails with Hope sustaining "the glorious mystery till our faith turns into sight." The hymns in this collection celebrate many of the names and images constantly revealing divinity: Love, Giver of Life, Creative Spirit, Wisdom, Loving Friend, Mother Eagle, Holy Beauty, Guide, Holy Spirit, Mother Hen, Holy Darkness, Healing Power, Loving Womb, Rock, Great Redeemer, Great Creator, Father, Mother, Brother, Sister, Resurrection Story, Spirit of Power, Mystery, Well of Freedom, Fountain, Source of All Creation, Faithful Friend, Midwife, *Ruah* (Hebrew word for "Spirit"), *El Shaddai* (Hebrew word for "God of the Breasts" or "God Almighty").

Inclusive Hymns for Liberating Christians is a collection that invites faith communities to open ourselves to new insights. Though no words can contain our great Creator, new words surprise us with new experiences of the divine within ourselves and others and beyond. Expanded concepts of divinity allow the fresh breath of the Spirit to move through communities.

Inclusive Language

All the language in these hymns is inclusive for humanity and for divinity. The hymns name women and children along with men, and balance masculine and feminine references to deity. Instead of "Rise Up, O Men of God," this collection includes hymns such as "Come, Sisters, Brothers, Come." Instead of "Eternal Father, Strong to Save," this collection includes hymns like "Father-Mother, Kind and Loving." Some of the hymns resurrect feminine images, like Wisdom and *Ruah*, that have long been buried in Scripture and Christian tradition. Bringing female sacred names into worship is vital to the revaluing of the feminine so that women may experience true equality and dignity. The ultimate end is a gender-balanced divine symbolism.

Most people still think of God as masculine and refer to God as "He." Because of centuries of association of "God" with male pronouns and imagery, this word generally evokes male images. Many of the hymns in this collection balance the noun "God" with feminine pronouns. I refer to God as "She" and "Her" not because I believe God is literally a woman, but in order to balance the masculine with the feminine. In addition, calling God "She" surprises us away from an unquestioning masculine naming of divinity. The Creator of the universe is both male and female and more. The Source of All cannot be limited to a single gender or a single set of metaphors.

Many of the hymns in this collection balance the masculine name "Christ" with the feminine name *Sophia* (word for "Wisdom" in the original Greek language of the Christian Scriptures). The name "Christ-Sophia" makes equal connections between male and female, and Jewish and Christian traditions, thus providing a model for a community in which all live in a partnership rather than a dominant-submissive relationship. Writers of Christian Scripture link Christ to Wisdom, a feminine symbol of deity in Hebrew Scripture. Wisdom (*Hokmah* in Hebrew) symbolizes creative, redemptive, and healing power. In their efforts to describe this same power in Christ, the apostle Paul and other Christian Scripture writers draw from the picture of feminine Wisdom in Hebrew Scripture. Paul refers to Christ as "the power of God and the Wisdom (*Sophia*) of God" (1Corinthians 1:24), and states that Christ "became for us Wisdom (*Sophia*) from God" (1 Corinthians 1:30). Proverbs describes *Hokmah* as the way, the life, and the path (4:11,22,26). The writer of the Gospel of John refers to Christ as "the way, and the truth, and the life" (John 14:6). What Judaism said of personified feminine Wisdom, Christian writers came to say of Christ: the image of the invisible God (Colossians 1:15); the radiant light of God's glory (Hebrews 1:3); the one through whom the world was created (John 1:3). In Matthew's gospel, Jesus identifies with Wisdom (*Sophia*): "the Son of Man came eating and drinking, and they say, 'Look, a glutton and a drunkard, a friend of tax collectors and sinners!' Yet Wisdom (*Sophia*) is vindicated by her deeds" (Matthew 11:19). See *In Search of the Christ-Sophia: An Inclusive Christology for Liberating Christians* (Twenty-Third Publications, 1995; Eakin Press, 2004) for an elaboration of the connection between Christ and *Sophia* (Wisdom) in Scripture and Christian tradition.

This collection, *Inclusive Hymns for Liberating Christians*, also supports the sacred value of people of color by changing the traditional symbolism of dark as evil and white as purity and holiness. Many hymnals still include the hymn "Whiter than Snow," which repeats this line over and over: "Now wash me, and I shall be whiter than snow." A pastor of an African Methodist Episcopal Church told me how appalled he was to hear the children in his church singing these words: "Who's that dressed in white? It must be the children of the Israelites. Who's that dressed in black? It must be the hypocrites turning back." In many hymns images of light carry positive connotations, while images of darkness carry negative meanings. The hymns in this collection symbolize darkness as creative bounty and beauty. For example, "O Holy Darkness, Loving Womb" images darkness as a sacred well of rich-est beauty. "Womb of All Creation Flowing" pictures darkness as a holy power giving birth to all creation.

The hymns in this collection include non-human, along with feminine and masculine, divine imagery. The goal is to affirm the sacredness of all races of women and men, girls and boys, and all creation.

Social Justice Themes

Social justice is a major theme of *Inclusive Hymns for Liberating Christians*. One hymn draws images from Amos 5:24: "Let justice roll down like waters, and righteousness like an everflowing stream." The first stanza of the hymn sounds this call to justice:

> Let justice like waters roll down on our land;
> Help us, Christ-Sophia, to join in your plan.
> Let righteousness like everflowing streams rise;
> Come fill and anoint us, O Spirit most wise.

Many traditional hymns sanction and perpetuate injustice through exclusively masculine references, symbolism of darkness as evil, and imagery that gives highest value to the able-bodied. Too often faith communities avoid the discomfort of naming oppression, thus discounting its existence in our lives and allowing it to go unchallenged. The hymns in this collection challenge sexism, racism, poverty, heterosexism, and discrimination against disabled persons. These hymns seek to give equal value to all people. The first stanza of "Come, Sisters, Brothers, Come" challenges faith communities to include everyone:

> Come, sisters, brothers, come, and take the path to freedom;
> With voices lifted strong, we sing a song of welcome.
> So many are left out by dogma's stifling creed;
> We open wide the door for all to come and lead.

Worship and social justice cannot be separated. Without justice, our worship rings hollow. The prophet Amos denounces those who offer sacrifices and songs in worship while oppressing people. God will not accept the offerings of those who "push aside the needy in the gate" (Amos 5:12, 22-23). Neither could She be pleased with hymns and other worship rituals that by their very language oppress people by excluding or devaluing them.

In the United States alone, every seven seconds a woman is battered. One in three women experiences some kind of abuse. Throughout the world, an estimated four million women and girls are bought and sold into prostitution, slavery, or marriage. Approximately sixty million girls are missing as a result of infanticide, neglect, or sex-selective abortions. Seventy percent of the world's poor are women. A theology that truly includes women as well as men can make a powerful contribution to a more just world. Imaging God as feminine, as well as masculine and much more, will contribute to the valuing of women and girls in the divine image.

Hymns form the heart of worship. Instead of sitting passively listening to a sermon or watching a baptism, we take an active part in hymn-singing. And the music engraves the words in our hearts. While all the words in worship are vital, words sung in worship especially contribute to injustice or justice. Hymns can be powerful models and teachers of fairness. We can sing change into reality. Hymns that include all women and men and children give sacred value to everyone and inspire us to just action.

Liberation

Liberation and social justice go hand in hand. Freedom, liberty, liberation—I love these words, and I love to sing them. The most joyful, victorious hymns in this collection sing of freedom. Liberation is a theme that runs through the majority of the hymns. One of the stanzas of "Wake Us All, O Christ-Sophia," for example, calls us to freedom from the bonds of all kinds of oppression.

> Guide us now, O Christ-Sophia, showing us your daring way;
> Poor, oppressed, and hungry people call out for our care today.
> Help us break the yokes of bondage, deep in us and all around,
> Freeing everyone to blossom in your rich and fertile ground.

Many of our songs in worship have kept us in bondage to the injustices in our culture. The act of singing new words in itself frees us from slavery to tradition. We may never realize how custom-bound we are until we introduce new hymns into our worship services. Though there may be opposition, freedom will ring through our new inclusive songs.

This hymn collection encourages freedom from sexism, racism, and other injustices. These hymns stir freedom to find our own voices, follow our call, develop our gifts, become all we're created to be. "We Sound a Call to Freedom" exults in the victory of freedom:

> We sound a call to freedom that will heal our broken land;

As the call rings out more clearly, violent forces will disband.
Prison doors will open; bonds will loosen by the Spirit's hand;
The truth will set us free.

Resurrection and Abundant Life

Resurrection and life are prominent themes of *Inclusive Hymns for Liberating Christians*. The central themes of the Christian faith are resurrection and abundant life: "if Christ has not been raised, then our proclamation has been in vain and your faith has been in vain" (1 Corinthians 15:14); "I came that they may have life, and have it abundantly" (John 10:10). Many traditional hymns glorify suffering and death. Though the intent may be to express gratitude for the Passion, they often inadvertently sanction suffering. Hymns on the crucifixion, if given too much prominence in worship, keep the focus of faith on death. For example, the most recent Baptist hymnal includes 97 hymns under the headings "Jesus Christ—Blood" and "Jesus Christ—Cross," and only 31 under the heading "Jesus Christ—Resurrection."

Christian faith proclaims abundant life and resurrection not only for Christ but for all creation. The image of all creation standing "on tiptoe, longing toward revealing light" in the hymn "Hope of Glory, Living in Us" draws from Romans 8:19-21: "For the creation waits with eager longing for the revealing of the children of God; for the creation was subjected to futility, not of its own will but by the will of the one who subjected it, in hope that the creation itself will be set free from its bondage to decay and will obtain the freedom of the glory of the children of God." The resurrection means hope for us and for all creation. The resurrection forms the foundation for our mission of reviving that which is dead. In "Hope of Glory" we sing: "Challenged by your resurrection, we find hope to make things new."

The hymns in this collection name the reality of pain, but they focus on the victory of beauty. Life, not death, stands forth as the purpose of creation. Though suffering and death come, often in the service of a just cause, life triumphs. "O Flower Blooming, Deep in Pain" celebrates the courage to blossom in the midst of oppression. I wrote this hymn before I saw the movie "Life is Beautiful." Then in the movie I saw Guido Orefice, played by Roberto Benigni, vividly illustrate this remarkable strength of life that overcomes even the unspeakable violence of the Holocaust. Guido, by the power of the stories he creates, turns the concentration camp into a place of liveliness and hope for his young son, Giosue.

Words create reality. We speak and sing things into existence. If we magnify resurrection in our hymns, we take part in the conquering of death by life. The image of Christ-Sophia in many of my hymns invites singers to bring back to life a biblical feminine divine image that has long been buried, thus symbolizing the restoration of all creation. For example, "Rise Up, O Christ-Sophia" sings of hope that this resurrection will "empower us to labor . . . our wars to cease." The last stanza of "Christ-Sophia Lives Today" proclaims the power of resurrection:

> Christ-Sophia rises glorious, Alleluia!
> All creation sings victorious, Alleluia!
> Hope springs forth, surprise abounds, Alleluia!
> Earth transformed with joy resounds, Alleluia!

New Creation

"See, I am making all things new" (Revelation 21:5). This scriptural declaration provides another major theme for *Inclusive Hymns for Liberating Christians*. The Gospel brings hope of resurrecting the dead and continually creating the new. The Christian faith promises "a new creation" in which "everything old has passed away," and "everything has become new!" (2 Corinthians 5:17) In this collection the hymn "Celebrate a New Day Dawning" proclaims, "We become a new creation, bursting open into light." The hymn "Sister Spirit, Brother Spirit" concludes with this line: "Now our voices join in shouting, 'Come and see all things made new.'"

Elizabeth Schussler Fiorenza in the book *In Memory of Her* reveals that the earliest Christian community was a discipleship of equals. It was a new creation, no longer bearing the stamp of the culture. This transformed community flowed from the words and actions of Christ. In choosing Mary Magdalene as the first witness of the resurrection, when the religion and culture of that day discounted the testimony of women, Christ started the revolution of gender equality.

The new creation did not stop with Christ. The new creation continues with us. Through speaking and singing new words in our sacred worship, we become a new creation and contribute to new creation in our world. The last two lines of the hymn "Do You Want to Be Healed?" pray for this transformation:

> Help us to claim your grace, old patterns to erase;
> Your new creation's sign, we will be; we will be;
> Your new creation's sign, we will be.

My hope is that the hymns in this collection will contribute to the new creation. An inclusive worship community called "New Wineskins" has given me enthusiastic support in the creation of these hymns. The mission of New Wineskins is to explore new ways of seeing divinity and interpreting Scripture so that the spiritual

16

gifts of everyone are equally valued and nurtured. The name "New Wineskins," coming from the metaphor in Matthew 9:17, describes our search for new language and symbols to proclaim the Gospel of liberation and shalom. We include feminine and masculine divine names and images to symbolize shared power and responsibility. We welcome people from various faith backgrounds and encourage the discovery and exercise of everyone's gifts. The hymn "Welcome New Wineskins" celebrates the part this community plays in the new creation by "giving the world new visions divine."

Partnership in Relationships

The hymns in this collection support shared power in relationships, instead of dominance and submission. The divine images in the hymns signify partnership: "Christ-Sophia," "Sister-Brother," "Father-Mother," "She-He." These balanced images form the theological foundation for partnership in all relationships, as expressed, for example, in these lines: "O Sister-Brother, sacred image, show us now the way to work together side by side, true partnership display." Pictures of humanity include "joining hands with one another," "equal partners around the table," "partners for all gifts to flower," "sisters and brothers side by side," "sisters and brothers hand in hand," "women and men and children as partners."

Many traditional hymns squelch partnership by singing only of brothers or of an exclusively masculine deity. For example, in "Let There be Peace on Earth," we find the line "With God as our Father, brothers all are we." Though the intended message is of bringing people together for the work of peacemaking, by excluding half of humanity this song inadvertently sanctions the injustice that hinders peace. We need to reflect partnership in the language of our worship and in all our actions in order to proclaim the Good News of liberation and shalom.

To convey a belief in a community of partners, the hymns in this collection also use plural, not singular, references to people. These hymns refer to "we" and "us," not "I" and "me." Instead of "Abide with Me," this collection includes hymns like "Our God will Carry Us." The hope is that these hymns will encourage people to become equal partners.

These hymns also promote partnership with non-human life in saving the earth. In "Celebrate a New Day Dawning," we sing of "clapping trees and laughing rivers" joining "our call to liberty," and of "leaping deer and soaring eagles" sharing with us earth's fullness.

Partnership with the divine is another theme of *Inclusive Hymns for Liberating Christians*. The hymns picture God not as distant, but as within and among us. The Creator is a loving Friend walking beside us, not an unfeeling Ruler in the sky. The hymn "Friend and Source of All Creation" affirms our partnership with Christ-Sophia in the liberating mission: "You have called us friends and partners in your work of love and peace, co-creators in your mission to bring captives full release." The last lines of "Rise Up, O Christ-Sophia" picture our joining in the divine creation: "You call us as your ministers, to serve with you on earth, to co-create a mystery, new life with you to birth."

The hymn "Our God is a Mother and a Father" celebrates female-male partnership in heaven and on earth:

> Come, sisters and brothers, come and dance with glee,
> Together we grow into all we're meant to be.
> By joining with God both She and He,
> We open a world more than we can see.

Hymn-Writing Process

In the Advent season of 1995, shortly after my book *In Search of the Christ-Sophia: An Inclusive Christology for Liberating Christians* came out, I began writing hymns. The multitude of masculine images in traditional Christmas carols pelted me like stones. For several years I'd been part of an Inclusive Worship Community that had gender and racial inclusiveness as our goal. We sang hymns with inclusive language written by Jane Parker Huber to familiar hymn tunes. But we found no Christmas carols with inclusive language, and certainly none with balanced feminine and masculine names for divinity. I began to wonder how I would have felt if I'd grown up singing "O come, let us adore Her." I'd written this line in a litany, but I found singing it even more empowering. Knowing people's resistance to changing a few words in hymn texts, I decided to write a whole new poem to the tune "Adeste Fideles." My first hymn, "O Come, Christ-Sophia," came quickly and joyfully. A week later I wrote "Christ-Sophia Now We Praise" to the tune of "Hark, the Herald Angels Sing."

In the following months and years, I continued to write hymns. Because I find hymn-writing so delightful, sometimes I write a hymn as a break in the midst of another writing project. And it thrills me to hear people enthusiastically singing these hymns, whether in a small community or a large congregation or a convocation. When a group of clergywomen sang some of the hymns, I heard exhilaration in voices and saw tears streaming down faces. Although these women had received the official blessing of their churches through ordination, several told me that singing hymns inclusive of feminine divine names gave them a deeper feeling of worth than they had ever experienced.

When I'm writing a hymn, I usually start with an idea or an image and then choose a hymn tune that suits it. Often the ideas come from my favorite biblical passages. Sometimes I start with a tune that I love but have quit singing because of its text with exclusive language and theology. For the next few weeks the tune plays in my mind day and night, over and over like a CD set on "repeat." The image or idea expands into lines that I fit to the meter and usually the rhyme scheme of the original tune.

In the process of writing a hymn I discover that some words that express my theology do not sing well. So I search and struggle for the best words to carry meaning and sound. I work out images, rhymes, and meters wherever I am—in the car, exercising, getting dressed in the mornings, waiting for elevators at the hospital where I'm a chaplain, standing in grocery store lines. My best lines often come when I let go to my subconscious mind and allow words to emerge in my dreams or when I'm too tired to work for them. Sometimes in a burst of inspiration, an image becomes a song.

Hymns I grew up with in *The Baptist Hymnal* had four stanzas, so I began by writing most of my hymns with four stanzas. Somewhere along the process, three stanzas felt more natural. Perhaps the traditional sacred symbolism of the number three kept emerging, or I remembered that the minister of music at my home church would often leave out a stanza, usually the third, to save time in the service. Because each stanza in each of my hymns is important to the whole poem, I didn't want a stanza left out.

This collection, *Inclusive Hymns for Liberating Christians*, comes to you with an invitation to join the creative adventure of singing these new hymns and possibly writing new hymns for worship. You may have gifts in composing words and music together, as Larry Schultz has done with "A Living Celebration of Christ's Love" and several other hymns in this collection. Or your gifts may be writing only music or only words. You may find that traditional hymn tunes aid the writing of texts by providing a structure and that familiar music helps people accept new words. Or you may enjoy the freedom of writing texts for a composer to write new music; I have worked in this way with Larry on some of the hymns in this collection.

Our prayer is that the hymns in this collection will inspire communities and individuals to take part in the new creation. In partnership with our Creator, we have given birth to these hymns. We pray that they will help give birth to liberation, justice, peace, and abundant life in our world.

1

Sister Spirit, Brother Spirit

1 Corinthians 12:31; Revelation 21:1-6

1. Sis - ter Spir - it moves a - round us; Broth - er Spir - it
2. Broth - er Spir - it calls us for - ward; Sis - ter Spir - it
3. Sis - ter Spir - it gives us pow - er; Broth - er Spir - it

joins in love; She and He to - geth - er danc - ing,
points the way; He and She to - geth - er clear a
ends all strife; She and He to - geth - er lead us

crowned with ho - ly Heaven - ly Dove. May we join this
path in - to a bet - ter day. May we walk this
to a spring of flow - ing life. May we drink this

dance of free - dom, mak - ing heaven and earth a - new;
path of jus - tice, break - ing down each wall of fear,
gift of heal - ing from a Giv - er wise and true;

Words: Jann Aldredge-Clanton
Music: Larry E. Schultz

SPIRIT DANCE
8.7.8.7.D.

The meaning of this hymn text can be enhanced as it is expressed by Choir (or Soloists) and Congregation in the following manner:

Measures 1-4:   Each "Sister Spirit" phrase is sung by Female Choir Voices (or Female Soloist).
    Each "Brother Spirit" phrase is sung by Male Choir Voices (or Male Soloist).

Measures 5-8:   All phrases are sung together by Female and Male Choir Voices (or Female/Male Duet).

Measure 9 to end: The Congregation joins Choir (or Duet) in singing.

1a Sister Spirit, Brother Spirit

1 Corinthians 12:31; Revelation 21:1-6

1. Sis - ter Spir - it moves a - round us; Broth - er Spir - it joins in love;
2. Broth - er Spir - it calls us for - ward; Sis - ter Spir - it points the way;
3. Sis - ter Spir - it gives us pow - er; Broth - er Spir - it ends all strife;

She and He to - geth - er danc - ing crowned with ho - ly Heaven - ly Dove.
She and He to - geth - er clear a path in - to a bet - ter day.
She and He to - geth - er lead us to a spring of flow - ing life.

May we join this dance of free - dom, mak - ing heaven and earth a - new;
May we take this path of jus - tice, break - ing down each wall of fear,
May we drink this gift of heal - ing from a Giv - er wise and true;

All our gifts will blos - som ful - ly as our dreams come in - to view.
Faith - ful to our sa - cred call - ing so that Good News all may hear.
Now our voic - es join in shout - ing, "Come and see all things made new."

Words: Jann Aldredge-Clanton
Music: William Moore

HOLY MANNA
8.7.8.7.D.

Come Now, O Wisdom

Proverbs 3:13-20

1. Come now, O Wisdom; we need your clear voice;
2. Come now, O Wisdom; abide in our souls;
3. Wisdom, more precious than rubies or gold,
4. Wisdom, your grace joins all heaven and earth;

Speak and awaken our hearts to rejoice.
Stir in us visions of life free and whole.
With you our graces forever unfold.
With you we labor, new life to give birth.

Gracious Creator of more than we know,
Wisdom, our pathway to justice and peace,
No fame or fortune with you can compare;
Come now, O Wisdom, our Midwife and Friend;

In your own image may we ever grow.
With you our dreams find their fullest release.
Pour out your blessings, so rich and so rare.
Open our hearts to your world without end.

Words: Jann Aldredge-Clanton
Music: Traditional Irish Melody

SLANE
10.10.10.10.

3 Let Justice Roll Like Flowing Streams

Amos 5:24; Isaiah 58:6-8

1. Let jus - tice roll like flow - ing streams, Re - viv - ing all cre - a - tion. As peace a - wak - ens hopes and dreams, Come, sing in cel - e - bra - tion. Let heal - ing spring forth ev - ery - where; Join hands, a - bun - dant life to share; Praise Sis - ter - Broth - er Spir - it.

2. Let right-eous-ness fill ev - ery land, All those op - pressed re - leas - ing. Let e - vil for - ces now dis - band, All hate and vio - lence ceas - ing. Come, help the poor and hun - gry ones, That love and jus - tice will be done; Praise Sis - ter - Broth - er Spir - it.

3. Let free - dom ring from shore to shore, Re - stor - ing ev - ery na - tion. As bonds are bro - ken ev - er - more, Come, sing with great e - la - tion. Re - joice, there dawns a glo - rious morn; A new cre - a - tion now is born; Praise Sis - ter - Broth - er Spir - it.

Words: Jann Aldredge-Clanton
Music: Bohemian Brethren's *Kirchengesang*, 1566

MIT FREUDEN ZART
8.7.8.7.8.8.7.

God Like a Woman Long in Labor Cries   **4**

Isaiah 42:9, 14

1. God like a wom - an long in la - bor cries,
2. God calls us all to join Her la - bor long,
3. God brings the for - mer things to pass from earth,

Feel - ing the pain of all earth's an - guished sighs,
Feel - ing the pain of all who suf - fer wrong,
Join - ing with Her new life we bring to birth.

Long - ing to bring forth jus - tice ev - er - more,
Strug - gling to end op - pres - sion and its woe,
Now we can feel cre - a - tion's pure de - light,

That joy and free - dom ring on ev - er - y shore.
That like a riv - er peace will free - ly flow.
And all the world shines forth in beau - ty bright.

Words: Jann Aldredge-Clanton
Music: Frederick C. Atkinson

MORECAMBE
10.10.10.10.

5 Rise Up, All People

Isaiah 55:12; Proverbs 3:13-17

1. Rise up, all peo - ple; let us work for peace;
2. Rise up, all peo - ple; let us now join hands;
3. Rise up, be - hold our vi - sion's full re - lease;

Our sa - cred pow - er in the world re - lease;
Come, let us work for free - dom in all lands;
Our Great Cre - a - tor leads us forth in peace;

Vio - lence and ter - ror no more will hold sway;
Strong res - o - lu - tion for the task we pray;
Moun - tains and hills shall burst forth in - to song;

Our Great Cre - a - tor calls us for this day.
Our Great Cre - a - tor shows us Wis - dom's way.
Trees clap their hands; all peo - ple sing a - long.

Words: Jann Aldredge-Clanton
Music: George W. Warren

NATIONAL HYMN
10.10.10.10.

Our Mother-Father God, We Praise Your Prophets Bold

Jeremiah 18:18-20; Matthew 5:9-12; 13:57; 23:37

1. Our Moth-er-Fa-ther God, we praise your proph-ets bold,
2. Our Moth-er-Fa-ther God, we praise your proph-ets strong,
3. Our Moth-er-Fa-ther God, your proph-ets we will be,

Who call for peace and lib-er-ty for young and old.
Who, filled with deep de-vo-tion, speak a-gainst the wrong.
In part-ner-ship to change the world so all are free.

Your proph-ets come to help the poor and those op-pressed,
Though of-ten scoffed and scorned, your proph-ets lead the way,
New vi-sions we will speak; new ven-tures we will dare;

Who through the vio-lence and a-buse cry in dis-tress.
Pro-claim-ing truth, in-spir-ing hope through night and day.
We'll join with sis-ters and with broth-ers ev-ery-where.

Words: Jann Aldredge-Clanton
Music: Traditional Hebrew Melody
      Transcribed by Meyer Lyon

LEONI
Irregular

7   O Great Creator, Loving Friend

Micah 6:8

1. O Great Cre - a - tor, Lov - ing Friend,
2. May we do jus - tice un - to all,
3. May we love kind - ness day by day,

May we join you, our world to mend.
O - pen - ing doors and break - ing walls.
Fol - low - ing your re - deem - ing way.

Help us walk hum - bly close to you, As
Give us your power that sets us free, As
Walk - ing with you, we bring to birth Your

you cre - at - ed us to do.
you cre - at - ed us to be.
glo - rious reign of peace on earth.

Words: Jann Aldredge-Clanton
Music: H. Percy Smith

MARYTON
8.8.8.8. (LM)

O Brother-Sister Spirit, Come

Isaiah 61:1; Luke 4:18; Galatians 5:22

1. O Broth-er-Sis-ter Spir-it, come;
2. O Broth-er-Sis-ter Spir-it, wise,
3. O Broth-er-Sis-ter Spir-it, true,

Bring us your heal-ing; make us one.
From your deep well our dreams a-rise.
Fill us with hope and vi-sions new.

With you we set the cap-tives free,
With you we break op-pres-sion's wall,
A peace-ful way with you we show,

As you cre-at-ed all to be.
And bring your Good News un-to all.
Where joy and kind-ness o-ver-flow.

Words: Jann Aldredge-Clanton
Music: William Gardiner's *Sacred Melodies*, 1815

GERMANY
8.8.8.8. (LM)

9

O Mother-Father of Us All

Hosea 11:3-4

1. O Moth - er - Fa - ther, of us all, Who nur - tures us each day, We hear your gen - tle lov - ing call And feel your com - fort when we fall; Show us your peace - ful way.

2. O Moth - er - Fa - ther, hear our prayer, And send us grace to heal; O lift us up with ten - der care, And give us pow - er that we dare New vi - sions to re - veal.

3. O Moth - er - Fa - ther, help us show Your love to ev - ery - one; And in your im - age may we grow, So that your kind - ness o - ver - flows, And jus - tice will be done.

Words: Jann Aldredge-Clanton
Music: Frederick C. Maker

REST (ELTON)
Irregular

Let Justice Like Waters Roll Down

Amos 5:24; Luke 4:18

1. Let jus-tice like wa-ters roll down on our land;
2. Pure wis-dom and jus-tice flow forth from your hand;
3. Come now, Christ-So-phi-a, with bless-ings and peace
4. O may we flow free-ly like wa-ters and streams

Help us, Christ-So-phi-a, to join in your plan.
With you as our guide e-vil forc-es dis-band.
To calm us and stir us, our vi-sions re-lease,
To heal and re-store bro-ken hearts and lost dreams.

Let right-eous-ness like ev-er-flow-ing streams rise;
Give us, Christ-So-phi-a, the grace to pre-vail
Good News for the poor and fresh sight for the blind;
A-wak-en us ful-ly to all we can be,

Come, fill and a-noint us, O Spir-it most wise.
O'er sys-tems and pow-ers that keep cap-tives held.
Your voice calls us on the op-pressed to un-bind.
Re-claim-ing our souls as we set peo-ple free.

Words: Jann Aldredge-Clanton
Music: Welsh Folk Melody

ST. DENIO
11.11.11.11.

11 Gather Us Under Your Warm Wings

Matthew 23:37

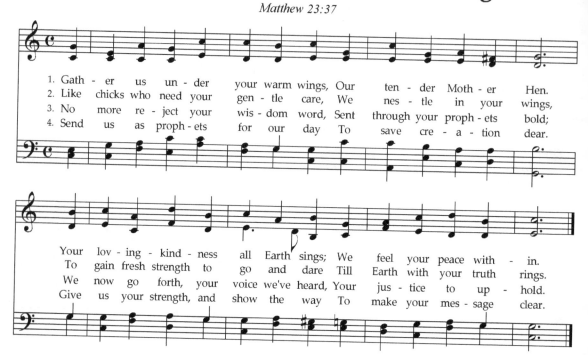

1. Gath - er us un - der your warm wings, Our ten - der Moth - er Hen.
2. Like chicks who need your gen - tle care, We nes - tle in your wings,
3. No more re - ject your wis - dom word, Sent through your proph - ets bold;
4. Send us as proph - ets for our day To save cre - a - tion dear.

Your lov - ing - kind - ness all Earth sings; We feel your peace with - in.
To gain fresh strength to go and dare Till Earth with your truth rings.
We now go forth, your voice we've heard, Your jus - tice to up - hold.
Give us your strength, and show the way To make your mes - sage clear.

Words: Jann Aldredge-Clanton
Music: William Croft

ST. ANNE
8.6.8.6.(CM)

Words ©1996 Jann Aldredge-Clanton.

O Come, Join Hands, All Violence Cease **12**

Luke 19:42; Ephesians 2:14; Proverbs 3:13-17; Isaiah 55:12

1. O come, join hands, all vio - lence cease, And fol - low Christ-So -
2. Come, heal di - vi - sions; break down walls, And lis - ten to the
3. Come, wom - en, men, and chil - dren now, As part - ners make a
4. The moun - tains and the hills shall sing, When peace through-out the

phi - a, our peace, Who bids us o - pen eyes to see The
Spir - it's calls To heal op - pres - sive sys - tems' blight, So
sa - cred vow To fol - low Wis - dom's paths to peace, And
world takes wing; The trees shall clap their hands in glee, As

ways that we make peace to be. A - rise, a - rise, feel
peace breaks through to give new sight.
teach Her ways of full re - lease.
joy bursts forth o'er land and sea.

joy in - crease; Come fol - low Christ-So - phi - a, our peace.

Words: Jann Aldredge-Clanton
Music: Plainsong; adapt. Thomas Helmore

VENI EMMANUEL
8.8.8.8. (LM) with Refrain

13 How Long, Christ-Sophia?

Proverbs 1:20-23; Psalm 74:3-7; Psalm 94:3-7; Habakkuk 1:1-4

1. How long, Christ-Sophia, how long must we wait?
   O when will the violence and suffering abate?
   The children are crying; O come to their aid;
   Our pleadings and prayers on your altar we've laid.

2. How long, Christ-Sophia, how long will it be
   Till justice will triumph so all can be free?
   O surely you feel all the anguish and pain;
   For you also suffer; rejected you've lain.

3. Arise, Christ-Sophia, and help us, we pray;
   With you we will labor to bring a new day;
   With you we will challenge the forces of wrong,
   Till we overcome with your love deep and strong.

Words: Jann Aldredge-Clanton
Music: Adonirum J. Gordon

GORDON
11.11.11.11.

Great Wisdom, Queen of All

14

Proverbs 1, 3

1. Great Wis - dom, Queen of all, Still sounds Her an - cient call
2. True Wis - dom in our hearts Jus - tice and peace im - parts,
3. Deep Wis - dom in our souls, From Her all good - ness flows

To paths of peace. When will we hear Her voice,
Her name we praise. Come feel Her heal - ing power,
Through - out our days. She is our dwell - ing place,

Make love and life our choice? Then na - tions
Flow - ing forth ev - ery hour; With Her our
Round us our sa - cred space; With us She

shall re - joice, All vio - lence cease.
spir - its flower; Her song we raise.
cel - e - brates Now and al - ways.

Words: Jann Aldredge-Clanton
Music: *Thesaurus Musicus*

AMERICA
6.6.4.6.6.6.4.

Join Now with New Power, Marching on for Peace

Matthew 5:9; Isaiah 58:6-7; Isaiah 55:12

* 1. Join now with new pow - er, march-ing on for peace;
2. Work to heal in - jus - tice; give the poor re - lief;
3. Then shall heal-ing spring forth as the dawn of day;

Broth - er - Sis - ter Spir - it leads our full re - lease.
Help the sick and lone - ly; com - fort those in grief.
Broth - er - Sis - ter Spir - it leads our joy - ful way.

We will not be daunt - ed by the force of greed;
Broth - er - Sis - ter Spir - it hears each pain - ful call;
Moun-tains join in sing - ing; trees shall clap their hands;

Come, let's work to - geth - er, meet - ing peo - ple's need.
We can join in help - ing break down ev - ery wall.
As we help in bring - ing peace through-out all lands.

Words: Jann Aldredge-Clanton
Music: Arthur S. Sullivan

ST. GERTRUDE
6.5.6.5.D. with Refrain

*Stanza 1 and each refrain should be sung in a brisk tempo.
The text of stanza 2 is enhanced as it is sung slowly and with freedom.
Stanza 3 should begin slowly and gradually increase in speed.

16 Wake Us All, O Christ-Sophia*

Isaiah 58:6-8, 11

1. Wake us all, O Christ-So-phi-a, by your lib-er-at-ing light;
2. Guide us now, O Christ-So-phi-a, show-ing us your dar-ing way;
3. Flow through us, O Christ-So-phi-a, reach-ing ev-ery des-ert place;

Stir in us the power and pas-sion, truth to speak and wrongs to right.
Poor, op-pressed and hun-gry peo-ple call out for our care to-day.
Fill us all with deep com-pas-sion as we claim trans-form-ing grace.

May we join your work of jus-tice; sis-ters, broth-ers side by side,
Help us break the yokes of bond-age, deep in us and all a-round,
Now we rise to go forth bold-ly, mak-ing dreams re-al-i-ty.

Bring-ing in your reign of splen-dor, doors of free-dom open-ing wide.
Free-ing ev-ery-one to blos-som in your rich and fer-tile ground.
Look, there dawns the glo-rious morn-ing; heal-ing springs up wide and free.

*Greek word for "Wisdom"

Words: Jann Aldredge-Clanton
Music: Franz Joseph Haydn

AUSTRIAN HYMN
8.7.8.7.D

Come, All Who Long for Peace and Justice on the Earth

Proverbs 1:20-23; 3:13-18; Revelation 21:5

1. Come, all who long for peace and jus-tice on the earth; Join
2. How long, how long must Wis-dom call be-fore we hear? For
3. The paths of Wis-dom lead to bless-ings deep and true; With

hands with Wis-dom, fol-low Her; Join hands with Wis-dom, fol-low Her; And
a - ges She has tried and tried; For a - ges She has tried and tried To
Wis - dom we will o - pen doors; With Wis - dom we will o - pen doors; And

bring new life to birth, and bring new life to birth.
make Her mes - sage clear, to make Her mes - sage clear.
see all things made new, and see all things made new.

A - wake now to Wis - dom; An - swer the call - ing of Wis - dom; Come

fol - low vi - sions of Wis - dom, Her beau - ti - ful vi - sions of peace.

Words: Jann Aldredge-Clanton
Music: Robert Lowry

Words ©2005 Jann Aldredge-Clanton.

MARCHING TO ZION
6.6.8.8.6.6. with Refrain

18

O Spirit of Power

2 Timothy 1:7; 1 John 4:8; 1 John 4:18

1. O Spir - it of Power, who dwells in us all,
2. Though man - y your names, Love reigns ov - er all,
3. O Spir - it of Love, com - pas - sion - ate Friend,
4. O Spir - it of Power, O Love be - yond thought,

In - spire us each hour to fol - low your call.
With you we can claim our life - giv - ing call.
With - in and a - bove, your strength knows no end.
Our gifts with you flower; what won - ders are wrought.

A - wak - en our vi - sion to all we can be
Cast out all our fear so with you we can soar,
Your riv - ers of heal - ing re - vive thirst - y land;
Cre - a - tor, Re - deem - er, and Com - fort - ing Guide,

And chal - lenge our lab - or to set peo - ple free.
Cre - at - ing a world nev - er dreamed of be - fore.
All good - ness and nour - ish - ment flow from your hand.
Il - lu - mine our lives as with you we a - bide.

Words: Jann Aldredge-Clanton
Music: Larry E. Schultz

SOARING SONG
10.10.11.11.

O Spirit of Power

2 Timothy 1:7; 1 John 4:8; 1 John 4:18

1. O Spir-it of Power, who dwells in us all,
2. Though ma-ny your names, Love reigns o-ver all;
3. O Spir-it of Love, com-pas-sion-ate Friend,
4. O Spir-it of Power, O Love be-yond thought,

In-spire us each hour to fol-low your call.
With you we can claim our life-giv-ing call.
With-in and a-bove, your strength knows no end.
Our gifts with you flower; what won-ders are wrought.

A-wak-en our vi-sion to all we can be,
Cast out all our fear so with you we can soar,
Your ri-vers of heal-ing re-vive thirst-y land;
Cre-a-tor, Re-deem-er and Com-fort-ing Guide,

And chal-lenge our la-bor to set peo-ple free.
Cre-at-ing a world ne-ver dreamed of be-fore.
All good-ness and nour-ish-ment flow from your hand.
Il-lu-mine our lives as with you we a-bide.

Words: Jann Aldredge-Clanton
Music: Adapt. from J. Michael Haydn

LYONS
10.10.11.11.

19 **Welcome Our Sister-Brother Creator**

Genesis 1; 2 Corinthians 5:17

Unison

1. Come, let us join our Sis-ter Cre-a - tor, Birth-ing a
2. Come, let us join our Broth-er Cre-a - tor, Bring-ing forth
3. Wel-come our Sis - ter - Broth-er Cre-a - tor, In - to our

new world more than we know. With Her re - veal - ing all of our
free - dom for ev-ery race. All of earth's col - ors danc-ing to-
spir - its' life-giv-ing wombs. Glad ex-pec - ta - tion grows from our

full - ness, We cre-ate heal - ing wher-e'er we go.
geth - er, Cel-e-brate beau - ty in ev-ery face.
la - bor For new cre-a - tion's glo-ri-ous blooms.

Words: Jann Aldredge-Clanton
Music: Traditional Gaelic Melody

BUNESSAN
5.5.5.4.D.

Great Friend of All People

John 15:12-15

1. Great Friend of all people, strong Sister and Brother,
2. Kind Sister and Brother, for - ev - er be - side us
3. True Friend and Com - pan - ion through all of our jour - ney,

We pray for your bless - ings and ten - der - est care.
To cheer and to guide as new mis - sions we dare.
Re - veal - ing new vi - sions of whole - ness for all.

May all lam - en - ta - tion be - come ex - pec - ta - tion
Your light in us flam - ing, with you we're re - claim - ing
Through our cel - e - bra - tion we join your cre - a - tion,

Of free - dom to cre - ate new life full and fair.
Our voic - es long de - nied and gifts rich and rare.
As part - ners we move on to an - swer our call.

Words: Jann Aldredge-Clanton
Music: Dutch Folk Song
     Harm. Edward Kremser

KREMSER
12.11.12.12.

21 Sister-Brother Spirit, Come

John 14:16-18, 26-27; Habakkuk 2:2-3

1. Sis - ter - Broth - er Spir - it, come To our long - ing minds and hearts.
2. Spir - it of all truth and grace, Deep with - in us al - ways stay.
3. Sis - ter - Broth - er Spir - it, come To all peo - ple ev - ery - where.

Vis - it us, O Ho - ly One, And your grace to us im - part.
Give us strength that we may face Ev - ery chal - lenge day by day.
Bring your peace to ev - ery - one, That your free - dom all may share.

Let your heal - ing wa - ters flow; Bring re - lief from pain and fear.
Help us break op - pres - sion's hold, As with you we la - bor long.
Shine your dream through ev - ery land; Make the vi - sion plain to see:

Give us hope that we may know Lov - ing care is al - ways near.
Keep us al - ways kind and bold, As we o - ver - come each wrong.
Men and wom - en join - ing hands, All your chil - dren safe and free.

Words: Jann Aldredge-Clanton
Music: Simeon B. Marsh

MARTYN
7.7.7.7.D.

Our God Is a Mother and a Father

22

Genesis 1:26-27; Isaiah 66:13; Psalm 103:13

1. Our God is a Moth-er and a Fa-ther too, And God is a Friend who will al-ways see us through. Our God is a Sis-ter who loves you and me, And God is a Broth-er who sets us free. God's im-age all are we, But our lov-ing God is more you see, For God who made both you and me, Is as great as great can be.

2. Come, sis-ters and broth-ers, come and dance with glee, To-geth-er we grow in-to all we're meant to be. By join-ing with God both He and She, We o-pen a world more than we can see.

Words: Jann Aldredge-Clanton
Music: Shaker Tune
     Arr. Larry E. Schultz

SIMPLE GIFTS
Irregular

Through Distant Lands and Over Stormy Seas

Psalm 139: 7-18

1. Through dis-tant lands and o-ver storm-y seas, keep us from harm;
2. With you the light and dark-ness are the same, sa-cred and whole;
3. Your works are won-der-ful be-yond com-pare, Spir-it most wise;

O Lov-ing Spir-it from us nev-er flee, shield from a-larm.
You move in all and call us each by name, calm-ing our souls.
With you cre-a-tive ven-tures we can dare and reach the skies.

Hold out your hand, and take a-way all fear;
Formed in your womb, we bear your im-age bright,
With you we go on wings of morn-ing light,

Give us fresh hope by your own pres - ence near.
Filled with your grace and pow-er day and night.
Find-ing new paths that lead through depths and heights.

Words: Jann Aldredge-Clanton
Music: John B. Dykes

LUX BENIGNA
10.4.10.4.10.10.

Rise and Speak Out

24

Proverbs 1:20-23; 3:13-18; Luke 4:18

1. When we look all a-round And see vio-lence a-bound, We are filled with dis-tress, fear, and doubt. Then we hear Wis-dom say "We can show a new way." And She leads us to rise and speak out.

2. There are those who con-demn Peo-ple dif-ferent from them; They a-buse and op-press with their clout. Wis-dom calls us to go, And Her kind-ness to show, And She leads us with love to speak out.

3. There'll be jus-tice and peace And the cap-tives' re-lease, When we wake up and hear Wis-dom shout. Then with Her we will dwell, And Her Good News we'll tell, For with Wis-dom we'll rise and speak out.

Rise up and shout, For it's time to speak out; Let us cry out with Wis-dom; Let us rise and speak out.

Words: Jann Aldredge-Clanton
Music: Daniel B. Towner

TRUST AND OBEY
Irregular

25 God Is She and He Together

Isaiah 55:8-9

1. God is She and He to - geth - er, And much more than we can know;
2. She and He to - geth - er give us Grace like o - ceans deep and wide;
3. All the ways of God are high - er than the heav - ens far a - bove;

As we o - pen minds and spir - its, Peace and jus - tice o - ver - flow.
All our gifts will ful - ly flour - ish As in free - dom we a - bide.
She and He to - geth - er lead us To a full - er, wid - er Love.

Words: Jann Aldredge-Clanton
Music: Lizzie S. Tourjee

WELLESLEY
8.7.8.7.

Holy Christ-Sophia*

Isaiah 6:3; Luke 4:18; Revelation 21:5

1. Ho - ly Christ So - phi - a, beau - ti - ful Cre - a - tor,
2. Bless - ed Christ - So - phi - a, mer - ci - ful Re - deem - er,
3. Might - y Christ - So - phi - a, gen - tle Ho - ly Spir - it,
4. Ho - ly Christ - So - phi - a, Trin - i - ty of Wis - dom,

Rouse us from our slum - ber - ing to make the world a - new.
Heal, re - store, and chal - lenge us to set all cap - tives free.
Sis - ters, broth - ers, side by side, join in your work of peace.
All cre - a - tion sings your praise in ac - cents wild and free.

Ho - ly Christ - So - phi - a, may we join your la - bor
You a - lone can save us by your voice with - in us,
Ho - ly Christ - So - phi - a, com - fort - ing and guid - ing,
Moun - tains bow be - fore you, pur - ple fields ex - tol you

To bring forth peace and all that's just and true.
Call - ing us on toward all we're meant to be.
Give us new hope and pow - er to re - lease.
For your pure grace, your true e - qual - i - ty.

*Greek word for "Wisdom"

Words: Jann Aldredge-Clanton
Music: John B. Dykes

Words ©1996 Jann Aldredge-Clanton.

NICAEA
Irregular

27

O Christ-Sophia, Holy One

Ephesians 4:15

1. O Christ - So - phi - a, Ho - ly One, We need your love and grace
2. O Sis - ter - Broth-er, Friend of all, Come show us now the way
3. Cre - a - tive Spir - it, dwell in us, and wak - en all our power,

To speak your truth and o - pen minds, The deep - est fears e - rase.
To work to - geth - er side by side, True part - ner - ship dis - play.
That we may join your dar - ing plan For all to ful - ly flower.

Give us faith, give us hope to cre - ate a bright-er day With your lib - er - ty and whole-ness for all.

We will dream and work and u - nite as we pray for cour - age to car - ry out our call.

Words: Jann Aldredge-Clanton
Music: Ralph E. Hudson

HUDSON
8.6.8.6. (CM) with Refrain

Awake to the Voice of Wisdom

Proverbs 1:20-25; Matthew 23:37; Luke 11:49-51

1. The whole world was ach-ing from vio-lence and greed, Ig-nor-ing the words of
2. She comes like a Moth-er with nur-tur-ing love, De-sir-ing to reach all
3. She comes through the words of the proph-ets so bold; A-wake to the voice of
4. Her proph-ets have nev-er been safe on this earth, But e-vil can-not de-

Wis - dom. How long, oh, how long must She suf-fer and plead? A-
peo - ple. She long-ing-ly calls from with - in and a-bove; A-
Wis - dom. Her mes-sage of jus-tice will nev-er grow old; A-
stroy us. With Wis-dom we la-bor for peace to be birthed; We've

wake to the voice of Wis-dom.
wake to the voice of Wis-dom. Come to Her now; She's cried out so long; Join-ing with Her, we
wake to the voice of Wis-dom.
heard the clear voice of Wis-dom.

o-ver-come wrong. Hear Wis-dom's call to sing a new song. A-wake to the voice of Wis-dom.

Words: Jann Aldredge-Clanton
Music: Philip P. Bliss

LIGHT OF THE WORLD
11.8.11.8. with Refrain

29 Creative Spirit, Strong and Kind

Luke 4:18; Acts 2:17

1. Cre - a - tive Spir - it, strong and kind, Help us all cap - tives to un - bind. When we see peo - ple in dis - tress, May we join you to heal and bless. O give us hearts to feel the pain Of those who in op - pres - sion wane.

2. Cre - a - tive Spir - it, help us dare To preach your Good News ev - ery - where, That all re - flect your im - age bright With gifts that shine forth day and night. Pour out your pow - er on us all, That we may break down ev - ery wall.

3. Cre - a - tive Spir - it, stir our souls With vi - sions of a world made whole. Il - lu - mine us with proph - et dreams, That from us flow your heal - ing streams. O give us grace that we may be As you cre - at - ed, wise and free.

Words: Jann Aldredge-Clanton
Music: John B. Dykes

MELITA
8.8.8.8.8.8.

Words ©2000 Jann Aldredge-Clanton.

Hark! Wisdom's Urgent Cry

Proverbs 1, 3, 4, 8

1. Hark! Wis-dom's ur-gent cry Rings out for all to hear;
2. Look, Wis-dom's out-stretched hands Point to long life and love;
3. Come to the Tree of Life; She hon-ors our em-brace.

Though scoffed and scorned She still draws nigh With mes-sage strong and clear.
Her grace pours forth through-out all lands A-round us and a-bove.
Her fruit our deep-est powers re-vive; She crowns us with Her grace.

A-wake and heed Her voice, De-struc-tive ways now cease;
How long will we re-fuse Her gifts so rich and free?
The Tree of Life stands tall; Her beau-ty fills the earth.

U-nite with Wis-dom, make a choice To go on paths of peace.
How long our bond-age will we choose in-stead of lib-er-ty?
Her ra-diant flow-ers nev-er fall; Her full-ness brings new birth.

Words: Jann Aldredge-Clanton
Music: George J. Elvey

DIADEMATA
6.6.8.6.D. (SMD)

31 Come, Father-Mother, Friend and Guide

Genesis 1:27; Isaiah 66:13; Isaiah 40:25; John 15:15; John 15:26; John 6:35;
John 8:12; Deuteronomy 32:18; 1 Corinthians 10:4; Mark 1:10

1. Come, Fa-ther-Moth-er, Friend and Guide; Giv-er of Life, with us a-bide.
2. Bread of new Life, our strength each day, Light of the World, show us the way;
3. Come, Broth-er-Sis-ter Spir-it wise; Join-ing with you our dreams a-rise.

O-pen our minds to all you pro-claim, O Ho-ly One of man-y names.
Rock of all a-ges on whom we stand, Give us fresh hope in wea-ry lands.
Made in your im-age, we can be free, Grow-ing to be all we can be.

Come with your heal-ing streams of Love, Mov-ing with-in us and a-bove;

Come, Ho-ly Spir-it, Heav-en-ly Dove, Pow-er Di-vine.

Words: Jann Aldredge-Clanton
Music: Clara H. Scott

SCOTT
Irregular

Come, Sisters, Brothers, Come

Galations 5:1, 13-14

1. Come, sis - ters, broth - ers, come, and take the path to free - dom;
2. For free - dom we are called to o - pen ev - ery pris - on;
3. O Sis - ter - Broth - er Love, in - dwell us with your full - ness;

With voic - es lift - ed strong, we sing a song of wel - come.
O may we bring re - lease to all who car - ry bur - dens.
May we your bless - ings spread, so all may know your whole - ness.

So man - y are left out by dog - ma's sti - fling creed;
No more will we sub - mit to chains that keep us bound;
Let noth - ing hin - der us from claim - ing all our power

We o - pen wide the door for all to come and lead.
We now stand firm and free; our voic - es we have found.
To make our vi - sions real, so all our gifts may flower.

Words: Jann Aldredge-Clanton
Music: Johann Cruger; Harm. Felix Mendelssohn   Words ©1998 Jann Aldredge-Clanton.

NUN DANKET
Irregular

33 Friend and Source of All Creation

John 15:12-15; Luke 4:18

1. Friend and Source of all cre - a - tion, free-dom flows forth from your love.
2. No more slave to sti - fling cus-toms, now cre - a - tive life can soar.
3. You have called us friends and part-ners in your work of love and peace,

May we feel your stir - ring pow - er, deep with - in us and a - bove.
You've made known all sa - cred Wis-dom, open-ing wide the hal-lowed door.
Co - cre - a - tors in your mis - sion to bring cap-tives full re - lease.

May we join you, Christ - So-phi - a, Mak - ing all the wound-ed
Give to us, O Christ - So-phi - a, Strength and grace to speak your
Give us now, O Christ - So-phi - a, Hope to make our vi - sions

whole, Mak - ing all the wound - ed whole.
truth, Strength and grace to speak your truth.
real, Hope to make our vi - sions real.

Words: Jann Aldredge-Clanton
Music: John Hughes

Words ©1999 Jann Aldredge-Clanton.

CWM RHONDDA
8.7.8.7.8.7.7.

O Christ-Sophia, Give Us Power   **34**

Luke 4:18; 1 John 4:18

1. O Christ-So-phi-a, give us power to work with you for right. We join you in this cru-cial hour to shine forth free-dom's light. We join you in this cru-cial hour to shine forth free-dom's light.

2. O Christ-So-phi-a, give us grace to show your peace-ful way. O bring to cap-tives full re-lease and Good News night and day. O bring to cap-tives full re-lease and Good News night and day.

3. O Christ-So-phi-a, give us love to cast out all our fear. O move with-in us and a-bove to free all far and near. O move with-in us and a-bove to free all far and near.

Words: Jann Aldredge-Clanton
Music: Oliver Holden

CORONATION
8.6.8.6. (CM)

Stir Us Out of Our Safe Nest, Mother Eagle

Deuteronomy 32:11-12

1. Stir us out of our safe nest; Moth-er Ea-gle, come near-by.
2. Take us up on your strong wings; Moth-er Ea-gle, give us flight;
3. Moth-er Ea-gle, send us out, Free-ly fly-ing on our own.
4. As with ea-gle's wings we fly, Leav-ing each con-fin-ing place.

Hold us close to your warm breast, While we learn to risk and fly.
Borne a-loft our spir-its sing, As we soar in-to your light.
Claim-ing all our gifts we shout, Glad to be at last full grown.
For fresh air and forms we cry, As we move out in-to space.

Lift us up with you, we pray; Help us see a bright new day.
Lift us up with you, we pray; Help us see a bright new day.
Soar-ing now with you, we say, "Look there dawns the bright new day."
Soar-ing now with you, we say, "Look there dawns the bright new day."

Words: Jann Aldredge-Clanton
Music: Conrad Kocher
     adapt. William Henry Monk

DIX
7.7.7.7.7.7.

Out of the Depths
Christ-Sophia Is Calling

John 10:10; Revelation 21:4

1. Out of the depths Christ-So-phi-a is call-ing, Call-ing from deep in our souls;
2. Long have we la-bored and hun-gered for bless-ing, Bless-ing of all we can be,
3. Deep in our souls Christ-So-phi-a is long-ing, Long-ing to calm all our fears,
4. Come and re-ceive Christ-So-phi-a's rich bless-ings, Bless-ings for you and for me,

Gent - ly the voice of true wis-dom and heal-ing, Calls us to rise and be
While all a-long our true voice has been call-ing, Call-ing in you and in
Com-fort our griev-ing and share all our strug-gles, Wip-ing a-way ev-ery
Peace for our jour-ney and hope for our vi-sion, Cour-age to set us all

whole. "Come home, come home," Hear Christ-So-phi-a's clear call;
me. "Come home, come home,"
tear.
free.

"Come to your full-ness of pow-er and wis-dom; Come home to life with-in you."

Words: Jann Aldredge-Clanton
Music: Will L. Thompson

THOMPSON
Irregular

37 Tread Lightly on Your Heavy Path

Psalm 23

*1. "Tread light-ly on your heav-y path; your spir-it can stay free;
2. "Tread gent-ly through the wea-ry maze; stay calm-ly clear and whole.
3. "Tread smooth-ly on the rug-ged edge; your strength will long en-dure;

Walk soft-ly past the fear and wrath; there's more in life to see."
With mead-ows green sur-round your days; deep peace re-stores your soul."
Move sure-ly o'er each crag and ledge; your steps will be se-cure."

We hear your gen-tle voice with-in, O Christ-So-phi-a, Friend;
We hear you, Christ-So-phi-a, Friend, for you our spir-its long;
Your words of com-fort light our way; O Christ-So-phi-a, Guide;

You lead us past the nois-y din, by wa-ters still you wend.
Your voice bids us our needs to tend; you fill our lives with song.
Your kind-ness o-ver-flows each day, as we with you a-bide.

*A solo voice sings the first two lines of each stanza; all sing the last two lines.

Words: Jann Aldredge-Clanton
Music: *Southern Harmony*, 1835

Words ©1996 Jann Aldredge-Clanton.

RESIGNATION
8.6.8.6.D. (CMD)

Our Mother-Father God Is Near

Matthew 6:25-34

1. Look, birds are fly - ing in the air, With - out a wor - ry nor a care;
2. Look at the lil - ies bright and fair; They live and grow with - out a care;
3. When wor - ries come to cloud our days, The birds and lil - ies show the way;

Our Fa - ther - Moth - er al - so gives Us all we need each day to live.
Yet they are clothed most splen - did - ly, And God pro - vides for you and me.
Like them we trust for ev - ery - thing, And find the peace that faith can bring.

Our Moth - er - Fa - ther God is near; We need not wor - ry,

need not fear; Our Moth - er - Fa - ther God is near.

Words: Jann Aldredge-Clanton
Music: William B. Bradbury

SOLID ROCK
8.8.8.8. (LM) with Refrain

Words ©2004 Jann Aldredge-Clanton.

Christ-Sophia, Wise and Fair

1 Corinthians 1:24-25

1. Christ-So - phi - a, wise and fair, May we know your trea - sures
2. Christ-So - phi - a, may we know That your pow - er through us
3. All by you are blessed and called, For you break down ev - ery

rare. O - pen wide our hearts and minds That your
flows. When our way is hard and long, Help us
wall. Christ - So - phi - a, help us show That your

wis - dom we may find. Guide us on your paths of
sing a hope - ful song. Give us strength when we are
gifts so free - ly flow. May we o - pen ev - ery

peace; Help us all our fears re - lease.
weak; Give us cour - age, truth to seek.
door By your grace for - ev - er - more.

Words: Jann Aldredge-Clanton
Music: Thomas Hastings

Words ©2000 Jann Aldredge-Clanton.

TOPLADY
7.7.7.7.7.7.

God Walks with Us

Psalm 23

1. God walks with us to cheer and guide, For - ev - er with us to a - bide;
2. Some - times our la - bor seems in vain, And bur - dened by a world of pain;
3. And when our path seems slow and long, She comes to us with hope-ful song;

Through ev - ery tri - al, ev - ery fear, God's lov-ing hand is al - ways near.
Though moun-tains quake and o - ceans roll, God's lov-ing pres - ence calms our souls.
Through val - leys deep, by wa - ters clear, God's lov-ing hand is al - ways near.

She walks be - side us all the way; She walks be - side us ev - ery day.

Her faith - ful part - ners we will be, For by Her grace She sets us free.

Words: Jann Aldredge-Clanton
Music: William B. Bradbury

HE LEADETH ME
8.8.8.8. (LM) with Refrain

41 O Holy Spirit, Mystery Within

John 14:15-17, 26-27; John 8:32; 1 John 4:18

1. O Holy Spirit, Mystery within,
2. Spirit of Love, come, fill us all today;
3. Spirit of Peace, come, still our troubled hearts;
4. Spirit of Truth, our Advocate and Guide,

O blessed Fountain, where new life begins,
Calm every fear, and comfort us, we pray.
Open our lives to healing you impart.
Help us to feel you always by our side.

Flow through the desert places in our souls;
Help us to feel ourselves in you secure,
Help us move toward our visions unafraid,
Teach us to speak your liberating Word,

As we drink deeply, make us free and whole.
That we may share your feast, so rich and pure.
As all our cares and griefs on you are laid.
And may your message through our lives be heard.

Words: Jann Aldredge-Clanton
Music: William Henry Monk

EVENTIDE
10.10.10.10.

Listen, Now We Tell a Mystery

1 Corinthians 15:51-54

1. Lis - ten, now we tell a mys-tery, told by proph-ets long be - fore;
2. Sound the trans - for - ma - tion trum-pet; sing a song of vic - to - ry;
3. Cel - e - brate new life e - ter - nal, spring-ing from Cre - a - tive Love;

We will all be changed for - ev - er; pain and death will be no more.
Heaven and earth join in the cho - rus, wel - com - ing new lib - er - ty.
Res - ur - rec - tion brings re - joic - ing all a - round us and a - bove.

With the Spir - it's heal - ing pow - er faith be - comes re - al - i - ty;
Ev - er chang-ing, ev - er grow-ing, we claim all we're meant to be,
With the lib - er - at - ing Spir - it, we will soar on an - gel wings,

We pro - claim im - mor - tal glo - ry far be - yond what we can see.
Join - ing in the Spir - it's work of set - ting all cre - a - tion free.
Ev - er on - ward, ev - er for - ward, as the world in tri - umph rings.

Words: Jann Aldredge-Clanton
Music: Ludwig van Beethoven

HYMN TO JOY
8.7.8.7.D.

43 O Wisdom in Our Hearts

Proverbs 2:10-11; Isaiah 42:14

1. O Wis-dom in our hearts, Your deep-est truth im-part;
2. O Wis-dom, keep us strong, When la-bor seems so long;
3. O Wis-dom, in us flow, That we may ful-ly show

Come, be our Guide. Show us your peace-ful way,
Keep hope a-live. On you we can re-ly
Your love-ly view. O bring your pow-er near,

Call-ing to us each day; O like a
To share each pain-ful cry, And bring your
That we may have no fear To speak your

shin-ing ray, In us a-bide.
com-fort nigh, Our dreams re-vive.
mes-sage clear Of life a-new.

Words: Jann Aldredge-Clanton
Music: Lowell Mason

OLIVET
Irregular

Love Rises Up

44

Luke 24:46-47; Hebrews 2:2-3

1. Love rises up from deadly foes,
   Healing divisions, pain, and woes;
   Our great Creator - Wisdom - Guide
   Leads to new life, so full and wide.

2. Hope springs from visions plain to see,
   Setting oppressive systems free;
   Our risen Sister - Brother - Friend
   Gives us new power, our world to mend.

3. Joy blossoms freely through all lands;
   Sisters and brothers, hand in hand,
   Bring new creation's dream to sight,
   Rising together into light.

Words: Jann Aldredge-Clanton
Music: John Hatton

DUKE STREET
8.8.8.8. (LM)

45

Come, Sister-Brother Spirit

Isaiah 11:6-9; John 8:32

1. Come, Sis - ter - Broth - er Spir - it to make our world a - new;
2. Come, Sis - ter - Broth - er Spir - it, for you the whole world longs;
3. Come, Sis - ter - Broth - er Spir - it to lib - er - ate all earth;

Your path of truth we fol - low to full - er, wid - er views;
We join your heal - ing mis - sion, your work of right-ing wrongs.
As part - ners we will la - bor to bring new life to birth.

All minds and hearts will o - pen with your trans - form - ing Love;
No more will hate and vio - lence your good cre - a - tion mar;
All crea - tures come to - geth - er to wel - come glo - rious days;

Pour out your grace and pow - er, O ho - ly, Heav - enly Dove.
For your re - deem - ing jus - tice we're spread - ing near and far.
The lion and lamb in peace dwell, and chil - dren lead the way.

Words: Jann Aldredge-Clanton
Music: *Gesangbuch*, Wittenberg, 1784

ELLACOMBE
7.6.7.6.D.

El Shaddai,* O Holy One

46

Genesis 49:25

1. El Shad-dai, O Ho - ly One, Might - y to de - liv - er,
2. Hold us close, O El - Shad - dai, Give us dear - est trea - sures,
3. Nour - ish us, O El Shad - dai, Keep us ev - er grow - ing,

Life a - bun - dant flows from you, Like a fer - tile riv - er.
Beau - ty to in - spire our dreams, Love be - yond all mea - sure.
That our gifts may ful - ly bloom As your grace we're show - ing.

El Shad-dai, El Shad-dai, Bless - ings on us show - er;

Bless - ings flow - ing from your love Bring new life and pow - er.

*Hebrew word translated "God of the Breasts," "the Breasted God," or "God Almighty"

Words: Jann Aldredge-Clanton
Music: William H. Doane

NEAR THE CROSS
7.6.7.6. with Refrain

47 Father-Mother, Kind and Loving

Matthew 6:25-30; 11:28

1. Father - Mother, kind and loving, Your a-bundance we're dis-cov-ering. You pro-vide and gent-ly nour-ish; Through your grace we ful-ly flour-ish.

2. Sis-ter - Broth-er, wise and car-ing, All our bur-dens you are shar-ing. Faith-ful Friend through joy and sor-row, You give vi-sion for to-mor-row.

3. Ho-ly Spir-it, in us liv-ing, Hope and pow-er you are giv-ing; From your well of wa-ter flow-ing Comes deep peace be-yond all know-ing.

Words: Jann Aldredge-Clanton
Music: Traditional Swedish Melody

TRYGGARE KAN INGEN VARA
8.8.8.8. (LM)

Womb of All Creation Flowing

48

Genesis 49:25; Isaiah 44:2-4

1. Womb of all cre - a - tion flow - ing with your bless - ings
2. Ho - ly Dark - ness deep with - in us, nur - ture our cre -
3. Lov - ing Womb, your sa - cred dark - ness brings forth trea - sures

ev - ery - where, Bring to birth in us deep car - ing
a - tive seeds; Bring our dreams to glo - rious flow - er
night and day, Nour - ish - ing our deep - est long - ings,

that your full - ness all may share. Fill us with your
as your peace our spir - its feed. In your cen - ter
cast - ing all our fears a - way. May we join your

gen - tle pow - er that new ven - tures we may dare.
we find whole - ness as your grace fills all our needs.
ho - ly la - bor, giv - ing Earth new hope, we pray.

Words: Jann Aldredge-Clanton
Music: Traditional French Carol

PICARDY
8.7.8.7.8.7

Rise Up, O People,
Proclaim Christ-Sophia Has Risen

Isaiah 60:1-5, Matthew 9:22

1. Rise up, O people, pro - claim Christ - So - phi - a has
2. Take heart, O daugh - ters, be - hold, Christ - So - phi - a brings
3. Come now, O sis - ters, and join Christ - So - phi - a in
4. Sing a new song and re - joice, Christ - So - phi - a a -

ris - en, Rais - ing the bur - ied and open - ing the
heal - ing; Sons, lift your eyes and find health in this
dar - ing. Broth - ers, join in and lay down heav - y
dor - ing. Glo - ry and free - dom with - in and a -

doors to all pris - ons. Rise up and shine! Light - ing the
sa - cred re - veal - ing. Claim life a - new! Earth's rich - est
bur - dens you're bear - ing. Come one and all! Fol - low the
round us re - stor - ing. Sing, for the light Comes to re -

path - way di - vine, As we de - clare this true vi - sion.
beau - ty re - new, Show - ing a way so ap - peal - ing.
life - giv - ing call, Chang - ing the world through deep car - ing.
vive truth and right; Now ra - diant spir - its are soar - ing.

Words: Jann Aldredge-Clanton
Music: *Erneuerten Gesangbuch,* 1665

LOBE DEN HERREN
Irregular

Our God Will Carry Us

50

Isaiah 46:3-4; Hosea 11:3-4

1. Our God will car - ry us Through all our
2. Our God for us pro - vides And feeds our
3. Our God is al - ways near To heal our
4. Our God who gave us birth Will see us

days; She gives us lov - ing care And with us stays.
souls; She lifts us up each day And makes us whole.
pain; Held in Her ten - der arms, New hope we gain.
through; She gives us ev - ery day Her life a - new.

Our God with us through life goes; Ev - er will Her love flow;

She nur - tures us and guides us to learn and grow.

Words: Jann Aldredge-Clanton
Music: Robert Lowry

NEED
Irregular

51 O Christ-Sophia, Rise

John 8:32, 10:10

1. O Christ-So - phi - a, rise; Come forth with strength a - new;
2. O Christ-So - phi - a, rise; Come forth with heal - ing grace;
3. O Christ-So - phi - a, rise; Come forth to end all strife;

Send out your Word to change our world And bring a wid - er view.
Send out your Peace to ev - ery land, And lib - er - ate each race.
Send out your Truth to set us free And bring a - bun - dant life.

A - rise, a - rise, Come forth with strength a - new.
a - rise, a - rise,

Words: Jann Aldredge-Clanton
Music: Arthur H Messiter

MARION
6.6.8.6. (SM) with Refrain

Words ©2001 Jann Aldredge-Clanton.

Celebrate a New Day Dawning

52

Isaiah 55:12

1. Cel - e - brate a   new day dawn-ing,   sun - rise   of   a   gold - en morn;
2. Christ-So - phi - a   lights the path-way   to   a   world of   har - mo - ny;
3. Sing   a   song of   ju - bi - la - tion,   dance with joy - ous   rev - el - ry;

Christ - So - phi - a   dwells a - mong us,   glo - rious vi - sions   now are born.
Sis - ter - Broth - er   Love sur-rounds us,   nour - ish - ing   our   syn - er - gy.
Clap - ping trees and   laugh - ing riv - ers   join our call to   lib - er - ty.

E - qual part-ners 'round the   ta - ble,   we make dreams re - al - i - ty;
Earth joins in our   rich com - mun-ion,   grate - ful   for   our   heal - ing care;
Free   at   last to   blos - som ful - ly,   flower - ing   forth   in   beau - ty bright,

Call - ing   out   our   gifts we nur - ture   hope be - yond all   we   can see.
Leap - ing deer and   soar - ing ea - gles,   all Earth's full - ness   now can share.
We   be - come   a   new cre - a - tion,   burst - ing   op - en   in - to light.

Words: Jann Aldredge-Clanton
Music: Ludwig van Beethoven

HYMN TO JOY
8.7.8.7.D.

53 Like a Mother with Her Children

Isaiah 43:1-2; 66:13

1. Like a Moth - er with her chil - dren you will com - fort us each day,
2. In your im - age you have made us, call - ing each of us by name,
3. With your vi - sion you in - spire us, giv - ing each a ho - ly call;

Giv - ing guid - ance on our jour - ney, as we seek to find our way.
Giv - ing strength for ev - ery chal - lenge as our gifts we ful - ly claim.
We will o - pen doors of free - dom by your pow - er in us all.

When we walk through fi - ery tri - als, you will help us take a stand;
We can hear you gent - ly say - ing, "Do not wor - ry, do not fear;
Life a - bun - dant spreads be - fore us as with ea - gle's wings we soar;

When we pass through trou - bled wa - ters, you hold out your ten - der hand;
For I'll al - ways go be - side you; ev - ery mo - ment I am near;
Join - ing in your new cre - a - tion, we re - joice for - ev - er - more;

When we pass through trou - bled wa - ters, you hold out your ten - der hand.
For I'll al - ways go be - side you; ev - ery mo - ment I am near."
Join - ing in your new cre - a - tion, we re - joice for - ev - er - more.

Words: Jann Aldredge-Clanton
Music: Robert Lowry

ALL THE WAY
8.7.8.7.D.

Creative Spirit, Come

54

Revelation 21:4-5

1. Cre - a - tive Spir - it, come, In - spire our work each day;
2. Cre - a - tive Spir - it, rise With - in us and a - bove;
3. Cre - a - tive Spir - it, come, And fill our world with peace;

As you are mak - ing all things new, Re - veal to us your way.
De - struc - tive forc - es lose their hold, Sur - round - ed by your love.
We join your lib - er - at - ing work, Your pow - er to in - crease.

Words: Jann Aldredge-Clanton
Music: *Genevan Psalter*, 1551 Edition
     Adapt. by William Crotch

OLD 134TH
6.6.8.6. (SM)

55 Loving Friend, Who Walks Beside Us

Psalm 143:8; Galatians 6:15

1. Lov - ing Friend, who walks be - side us, giv - ing strength for ev - ery day,
2. Help us claim our full - est pow - er, bring - ing free - dom un - to all;
3. May we join your new cre - a - tion, fill - ing earth with life a - new;

May your word of wis-dom guide us, as we seek your peace-ful way.
May our gifts and grac - es flow - er, as we break through ev - ery wall.
We will sing in cel - e - bra - tion of each love - ly shape and hue.

Like the dawn-ing of the morn-ing, fill our hearts with hope, we pray;
Great Re - deem - er, close be - side us, we can hear your lov - ing call;
Gra - cious Giv - er of all bless-ings, show us your wide o - pen view;

Like the dawn-ing of the morn-ing, fill our hearts with hope, we pray.
Great Re - deem - er, close be - side us, we can hear your lov - ing call.
Gra - cious Giv - er of all bless-ings, show us your wide o - pen view.

Words: Jann Aldredge-Clanton
Music: William B. Bradbury

BRADBURY
8.7.8.7.D.

Words ©2000 Jann Aldredge-Clanton.

Be Still and Know

Psalm 46:10; 104:30; 1 Corinthians 3:16

1. Be still and know that Ru - ah* dwells with - in;
2. Be still and know with Ru - ah we a - bide;

Spir - it of Power, She lives in us each day,
Spir - it of Life, with Her we can cre - ate

Giv-ing us strength new ven-tures to be - gin, And calm-ing
Beau-ty and peace to send out far and wide, Re - new-ing

all our fears a - long the way. Be still and know our mes-sage will be
earth as all with long - ing wait. Be still and know our vi-sions will come

heard, For She through us pro - claims the peace - ful Word.
true, For She gives hope to make cre - a - tion new.

*Hebrew word for "Spirit"

Words: Jann Aldredge-Clanton
Music: Jean Sibelius   Arr. Larry E. Schultz

FINLANDIA
10.10.10.10.10.10.

57 **Welcome New Wineskins**

Matthew 9:17

1. Wel - come new wine-skins, filled with new wine; Wel-come new vi-sions and sto - ries di-
2. Come and dis - cov - er Wis-dom ig - nored, Treasures and tal-ents too long un - ex-
3. Sis - ters and broth-ers e - qual - ly share, Work-ing as part-ners to dream and to

vine. Old forms and sym - bols nev - er will hold All of our gifts that dai - ly un - fold.
plored. Come to a place where all can be - long; Join in a new com-mu - ni - ty song.
dare. For a new peace and free-dom we pray, Join-ing our hands to bring a new day.

Welcome new wine-skins, filled with new wine, Giv-ing the world new vi-sions di - vine;

Welcome new wine-skins, filled with new wine, Giv-ing the world new vi-sions di - vine.

Words: Jann Aldredge-Clanton
Music: Phoebe Palmer Knapp

ASSURANCE
Irregular

Creator God of Many Names

58

Genesis 1:1-2; Isaiah 55:9; 1 Corinthians 1:24, 30; and Revelation 21:5.

1. Cre - a - tor God of man - y names, Give us your wid - est view;
2. Cre - a - tor God of man - y names, Give us your lov - ing care;
3. Cre - a - tor God of man - y names, Give us your deep - est grace;

We seek your Spir - it none can tame, Your vi - sions bright and new.
We seek your full - est gifts to claim, New dreams with you to dare.
We seek you more than wealth or fame, Your jus - tice for each race.

O Fa - ther - Moth - er, Friend to all, So - phi - a,* Ru - ah,* Guide,

In man - y names you come and call, In man - y names a - bide.

*Sophia is the Greek word for "Wisdom," linked to Christ in the Christian Scriptures.
*Ruah is the Hebrew word for "Spirit" in the book of Genesis and elsewhere in the Hebrew Scriptures.
**Cue-sized notes may be sung on the final stanza.

Words: Jann Aldredge-Clanton
Music: Larry E. Schultz

ALDREDGE-CLANTON
8.6.8.6.D. (CMD)

59   Christ-Sophia, Well of Freedom

Isaiah 55:1-3; John 10:10

1. Christ-So - phi - a, Well of Free - dom, may your springs of heal - ing flow
2. Christ-So - phi - a, Feast of Free - dom, may we claim your gifts to - day;
3. Christ-So - phi - a, Song of Free - dom, may we hear your mes - sage fair;

Through the moun-tains and the val - leys, so that all may ful - ly grow.
New ad - ven - tures spread be - fore us, call-ing to a bold - er way.
Set us free from all that binds us so our mu - sic fills the air.

Come we thirst - y to your wa - ters, long-ing for your gift of life.
Come we hun - gry to your ta - ble, long-ing for your Bread of Life;
Come we hope - ful through the strug - gle, long-ing for your gen - tle voice;

Si - lence all op - pres-sive voic - es; o - ver - come deep fear and strife.
Give us strength for trans-for - ma - tion, dar-ing dreams in us re - vive.
May we join your new cre - a - tion as all heaven and earth re - joice.

Words: Jann Aldredge-Clanton
Music: *The Sacred Harp*, 1844

NETTLETON
8.7.8.7.D.

Come, Weak and Weary Ones

60

Matthew 11:28-30; Luke 2:14

1. Come, weak and weary ones, heav-y with la-bor;
2. Sis-ters and broth-ers, come, gath-er with sing-ing;
3. O Moth-er - Fa-ther God, we join your la-bor,

Come to the arms of Love, ten-der and strong;
Come to the Well of Love; drink deep and long;
Work-ing with you to bring new life to birth;

Here we lay bur-dens down, deep com-fort sa-vor;
Here we as part-ners come, new vi-sions bring-ing;
O may we feel your grace, held in your fa-vor;

All pain and strug-gle will turn in-to song.
All pain and strug-gle will turn in-to song.
We join the an-gels to sing peace on earth.

Words: Jann Aldredge-Clanton
Music: Samuel Webbe

CONSOLATOR
11.10.11.10.

61 Are You Good and Are You Strong?

Psalm 42

1. Are you good and are you strong?
2. Why don't you stop all the pain?
3. Are you there and do you care?
4. Do you love us come what may?

Is it true you do no wrong?
Calm the fear and ease the strain?
Can we find you ev - ery - where?
Will you with us al - ways stay?

For some an - swers our hearts long.
For some an - swers our hearts long.
Can you help us when we fall?
Keep us safe - ly from all harm.

Unison

Like a child we sing this song.
Like a child we sing this song.
Do you hear us when we call?
Rock us gent - ly in your arms.

Words: Jann Aldredge-Clanton
Music: Larry E. Schultz & Jann Aldredge-Clanton

THEODICY
7.7.7.7.

God Like a Mother Comes Tenderly Near 62

Isaiah 66:13, 49:15

1. God like a Moth - er comes ten - der - ly near,
2. Nev - er for - get - ting us, al - ways close by,
3. Wel - com - ing ev - ery-one, arms o - pen wide,

Bring - ing new hope to us, calm - ing all fear.
God holds us to Her breast, hear - ing each sigh.
God like a Moth - er comes near - by to guide.

And through our griev - ing tears, Her gen - tle voice we hear,
On Her we can re - ly; She will our needs sup - ply,
She's al - ways on our side, ev - er with us a - bides,

God like a Moth - er comes ten - der - ly near.
Nev - ver for - get - ting us, al - ways close by.
Wel - com - ing ev - ery - one, arms o - pen wide.

Words: Jann Aldredge-Clanton
Music: Lowell Mason

BETHANY
6.4.6.4.6.6.6.4.

63   **Our Mother-Father Cares**

Psalm 57:1-10

1. When all a-round the tem-pests blow, Our Moth-er-Fa - ther cares;
2. As we are feel - ing pain and grief, Our Moth-er-Fa - ther cares;
3. As we are seek - ing peace-ful ways, Our Moth-er-Fa - ther cares.

Keep-ing us safe from ev - ery foe, Our Moth-er - Fa - ther cares.
Draw-ing us close to bring re-lief, Our Moth-er - Fa - ther cares.
Send-ing us stead - fast love each day, Our Moth-er - Fa - ther cares.

Our Moth - er - Fa - ther cares, Hold-ing us near, calm-ing each fear.

Our Moth - er - Fa - ther cares, All of our hopes to share.

Words: Jann Aldredge-Clanton
Music: W. Stillman Martin

GOD CARES
8.6.8.6. (CM) with Refrain

O Sister-Brother Spirit, Rise

Romans 8:19-23; Luke 4:18

1. O Sis-ter-Broth-er Spir-it, rise, And bring your heal-ing pow-er;
2. O Sis-ter-Broth-er Spir-it, hear Our cries for heal-ing pow-er;
3. The world is long-ing for your peace, Your full trans-form-ing pow-er;

Your lov-ing pres-ence, strong and wise, Will give us heal-ing pow-er.
So weak and wound-ed we draw near To touch your heal-ing pow-er.
With you all cap-tives find re-lease, Your free-ing, heal-ing pow-er.

Streams of heal-ing through us flow, As your hope with-in us grows;

Breathe new life in-to our world, Sis-ter-Broth-er Spir-it.

Words: Jann Aldredge-Clanton
Music: John H. Stockton

GREAT PHYSICIAN
8.7.8.7. with Refrain

65 God Like a Mother Hen

Psalm 17:8-9, 36:7; Matthew 23:37

1. God like a Moth - er Hen comes to our side;
2. God like a Moth - er Hen gath - ers us near,
3. God like a Moth - er Hen helps us to grow,

Un - der Her wings of love may we a - bide.
Hold - ing us to Her breast, calm - ing our fear.
Call - ing us long - ing - ly, jus - tice to show.

Shel - ter - ing from the storm, She keeps us safe and warm,
Giv - ing us dai - ly care, She will our sor - row share;
Her proph - ets we will be, set - ting all peo - ple free;

Through ev - ery day, our Friend and Guide.
Through ev - ery night, Her voice we hear.
Through ev - ery land, kind - ness will flow.

Words: Jann Aldredge-Clanton
Music: James H. Fillmore

PURER IN HEART
Irregular

Our God Like a Mother Will Come

66

Isaiah 66:13, 43:1-2

1. Our God like a Moth-er will come With Her com-fort gent-ly ca-ress-ing,
2. Our God like a Moth-er will come, When we pass through wa-ters of griev-ing;
3. Our God like a Moth-er will come, As new dreams with-in us are grow-ing;

Hold-ing out Her hand through each lone-ly land, And giv-ing us Her bless-ing.
In each doubt and fear, She is al-ways near To help us keep be-liev-ing.
Walk-ing by our side, She will sure-ly guide With wis-dom o-ver-flow-ing.

God goes with us through all our joys and tears; Ev-ery mo-ment She draws us near,

Giv-ing hope and com-fort a-long the way, And with us for-ev-er stays.

Words: Jann Aldredge-Clanton

Music: C. Austin Miles

GARDEN
Irregular

67 With Arms of Comfort God Comes Near

Isaiah 66:13; Psalm 131:2; 2 Corinthians 1:3-4

1. With arms of com-fort God comes near, And as a Moth-er calms her child, She wipes a-way all of our tears, And tells us we need have no fear Of harm through tem-pests wild.

2. God holds us close-ly to Her breast, And all our cares on Her we lay; She gives us ten-der love and rest, And goes with us on ev-ery quest To find a full-er way.

3. God's com-fort gives us strength to go To com-fort oth-ers in dis-tress; Her grace through us will o-ver-flow To bring more heal-ing than we know, And to for-ev-er bless.

Words: Jann Aldredge-Clanton
Music: Albert L. Peace

ST. MARGARET
Irregular

Come, Christ-Sophia, Healing Power **68**

2 Corinthians 1:3-5

1. Come, Christ - So - phi - a, heal - ing power;
2. Come, Christ - So - phi - a, give your hand
3. You calm our fears; you ease our pain;
4. Come, Christ - So - phi - a, power who heals;

Your grace all earth ex - tols;
To wipe our weep - ing eyes;
You heal our trou - bled hearts.
You make the wound - ed whole;

Your touch can make our spir - its flower;
Our sor - rows you can un - der - stand;
Your voice bids us new life to gain;
Your sa - cred name cre - a - tion fills

Your love re - stores our souls.
You feel our deep - est cries.
Your name deep peace im - parts.
With hope and health and joy.

Words: Jann Aldredge-Clanton
Music: *Virginia Harmony*, 1831   harm. Edwin O. Excell   Words ©1996 Jann Aldredge-Clanton.

NEW BRITAIN
8.6.8.6. (CM)

69 Share Our Grief, O Christ-Sophia

Psalm 30:5; 2 Corinthians 1:3-5; Revelation 21:4

1. Share our grief, O Christ-So-phi - a; Hear our cries, and feel our pain.
2. Wipe our tears, O Christ-So-phi - a; Heal our wounds; as - suage our grief.
3. Give us now, O Christ-So-phi - a, Kind-ness and con - sol - ing grace.

Sor - row's clouds hang dark a - round us; Heav - y tears flow down like rain.
Death and mourn - ing will be o - ver; Cry - ing eyes will find re - lief.
As we share your ten - der com - fort, We be - hold your bless - ed face.

Weep-ing en-dures while the long night pass - es; Joy dawns a-gain with the morn-ing light.

New life blooms through dust and ash - es; Hope re-born, we gain fresh sight.

Words: Jann Aldredge-Clanton
Music: William Walker's *Southern Harmony*, 1835

RESTORATION
8.7.8.7. with Refrain

Come to Me, All You with Heavy Hearts 70

Matthew 11:28-30; Proverbs 3:17-18

"Come un-to me, you wea-ry ones, And I will give you rest;

Come, leave your bur - dens in my arms, And lean up-on my breast." *Fine*

1. We hear you, Christ - So - phi - a; Our heav - y hearts re - joice
2. We la - bor, Christ - So - phi - a, To bring your truth to light;
3. You call us, Christ - So - phi - a, Our spir - its to re - vive;

D.C. al Fine

To bring our cares un - to you, And heed your gen - tle voice.
We of - ten feel dis - cour-aged When wrong pre - vails o'er right.
We learn from you the wis-dom To keep our hope a - live.

*Highlighting this hymn's dialogue, a male/female duet, expressing the voice of Christ-Sophia, may sing the refrain, with all other worshipers responding in singing the stanzas. (The duet may sing the unison melody, or in two parts with the male voice singing Tenor and the female voice singing Soprano.)

Words: Jann Aldredge-Clanton
Music: African-American Spiritual

BALM IN GILEAD
7.6.7.6.with Refrain

71 Hear Our Prayer, O Christ-Sophia

Mark 4:35-41

1. Hear our prayer, O Christ-So-phi-a; hold us in your lov-ing arms;
2. Through the storm we hear you call-ing in a voice so strong and clear,
3. Come with us, O Christ-So-phi-a, close be-side us al-ways stay;

Calm the storms that rage a-round us; keep us safe-ly from all harm.
"Have no fear for I'll be with you; peace, be still, for I am here."
In the midst of ev-ery strug-gle, guide us to your peace-ful way.

Do you care when we are sink-ing, tossed a-bout by wind and waves?
All at once your peace sur-rounds us, and the tu-mult is no more.
Give us cour-age for each chal-lenge; give us hope to dream and dare.

Can you still the wild-est tem-pest? Do you have the power to save?
Now the winds have ceased their rag-ing, and the waves no long-er roar.
Dear-est Friend through-out our jour-ney, show us trea-sures ev-ery-where.

Words: Jann Aldredge-Clanton
Music: Charles C. Converse

CONVERSE
8.7.8.7.D.

We Praise Our God of Many Names   **72**

Isaiah 66:13; John 15:15; John 4:10; John 6:35; 1 Corinthians 1:21-24

1. We praise our God of man-y names;
2. The Liv-ing Wa-ter in us flows;
3. Our Sis-ter-Broth-er Spir-it calls

Our Great Cre-a-tor we pro-claim;
The Bread of Life helps us to grow;
With words of peace to break down walls;

Our Moth-er, Fa-ther, Friend and Guide
The Christ-So-phi-a will a-bide
The Ho-ly Spir-it, Heaven-ly Dove

Walks with us al-ways by our side.
Where minds and hearts are o-pen wide.
Will fill us with a-bun-dant Love.

Words: Jann Aldredge-Clanton
Music: Thomas Tallis

TALLIS' CANON
8.8.8.8. (LM)

73 A Living Celebration of Christ's Love

Matthew 22:37-40

1. In faith we come to - geth - er, Christ's Bo - dy in the world,
2. With minds at - tuned and o - pened, we stud - y, seek - ing truth,
3. With o - pened arms of friend - ship, out - stretched, em - brac - ing all,
4. With bless - ing and com - mis - sion, The Spir - it sends us forth

our love to God ex - press - ing in ac - tion, sign and word,
the Truth re - vealed in Je - sus, to show our - selves ap - proved;
we wel - come friend or strang - er, re - spond - ing to Christ's call.
for ser - vice and for mis - sion a - round our street and earth.

to Wor - ship God, our high - est goal, in which we seek to
Dis - ci - ple - ship, our learn - ing quest, in - forms us how to
Through Fel - low - ship, our warm em - brace, we tan - gi - bly can
In Min - is - try, our car - ing task, we work, and prove to

be A Liv - ing Cel - e - bra - tion of Christ's Love.
be A Liv - ing Cel - e - bra - tion of Christ's Love.
be A Liv - ing Cel - e - bra - tion of Christ's Love.
be A Liv - ing Cel - e - bra - tion of Christ's Love.

*Cue-sized notes and other harmony may be sung on final stanza.

Words and Music: Larry E. Schultz

GRACE STREET
Irregular

O Mother-Father God

74

Psalm 19:1-6; Hebrews 13:5; Revelation 21:4

1. O Moth-er-Fa-ther God, your love sur-rounds us all;
2. O Moth-er-Fa-ther God, your beau-ty fills the earth;
3. O Moth-er-Fa-ther God, the heav-ens sing your praise;

Through rus-tling wind and spar-kling glen, we hear your gen-tle call.
From morn-ing light to star-ry night, you bring new life to birth.
All earth joins in the glo-rious hymn; a grate-ful song we raise.

With strong and ten-der care, you nur-ture us each day;
The fields in rain-bow hue are bloom-ing ev-ery-where,
Your grace ex-ceeds all thought, em-brac-ing ev-ery-one;

You calm our fears and wipe our tears, and with us al-ways stay.
While ro-bins sing to wel-come spring, and fra-grance fills the air.
Your kind-ness flows more than we know, from dawn to set-ting sun.

Words: Jann Aldredge-Clanton
Music: Franklin L. Sheppard

TERRA PATRIS
6.6.8.6.D.

75   O Great Creator

Psalm 139:9-18

1. O Great Cre - a - tor, Faith - ful Friend, lov - ing us more than
2. Wings of the morn - ing we will take, fol - low - ing you on
3. Dai - ly we praise your won - drous works, love - ly be - yond all

we can know, O hold us fast with ten - der hand,
ven - tures bold; Dark - ness and light are one with you;
words to tell; Formed in your im - age we will be

walk - ing with us wher - ev - er we go. O Great Cre - a - tor,
all day and night your gifts un - fold. O Great Cre - a - tor,
with you for - ev - er - more to dwell. O Great Cre - a - tor,

Faith - ful Friend, mar - vel - ous love to all you send.
Faith - ful Friend, mar - vel - ous love to all you send.
Faith - ful Friend, mar - vel - ous love to all you send.

Words: Jann Aldredge-Clanton
Music: Henri F. Hemy, James G. Walton

ST. CATHERINE
8.8.8.8.8.8.

Genesis 1

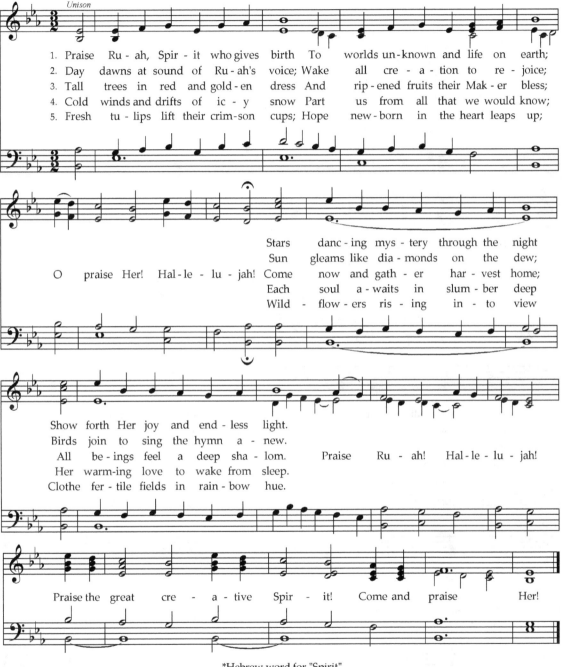

1. Praise Ru - ah, Spir - it who gives birth To worlds un-known and life on earth;
2. Day dawns at sound of Ru - ah's voice; Wake all cre - a - tion to re - joice;
3. Tall trees in red and gold - en dress And rip - ened fruits their Mak - er bless;
4. Cold winds and drifts of ic - y snow Part us from all that we would know;
5. Fresh tu - lips lift their crim-son cups; Hope new - born in the heart leaps up;

Stars danc - ing mys - tery through the night
Sun gleams like dia - monds on the dew;
O praise Her! Hal - le - lu - jah! Come now and gath - er har - vest home;
Each soul a - waits in slum - ber deep
Wild - flow - ers ris - ing in - to view

Show forth Her joy and end - less light.
Birds join to sing the hymn a - new.
All be - ings feel a deep sha - lom. Praise Ru - ah! Hal - le - lu - jah!
Her warm-ing love to wake from sleep.
Clothe fer - tile fields in rain - bow hue.

Praise the great cre - a - tive Spir - it! Come and praise Her!

Hebrew word for "Spirit"

Words: Jann Aldredge-Clanton; St. 4, Karen Ivy
Music: *Geistliche Kirchengesäng*, 1623; Arr. Larry E. Schultz

LASST UNS ERFREUEN
Irregular

77

Come, Holy Beauty

Genesis 1:26-27; Romans 8:19-23

1. Come, Ho-ly Beau-ty, stir our full hu-man-i-ty,
2. Come, Christ-So-phi-a, heal all wound-ed na-ture,
3. Come, Ho-ly Spir-it, fill us with your wis-dom.
4. Come, Ho-ly Beau-ty, wak-en our di-vin-i-ty,

That we may know we em-bod-y you.
That suf-fers long in grief and woe,
O-pen our eyes that we may see
That we may be your im-age fair,

All our di-ver-si-ty mir-rors your truth and grace;
Scarred by our care-less hands, cries out to thrive a-gain,
Splen-dor and ho-li-ness in ev-ery blade of grass,
Clothed in your dig-ni-ty, wis-dom, and lib-er-ty,

All rac-es show your love-ly hue.
To blos-som fresh, your ra-diance show.
The small-est crea-ture's maj-es-ty.
Cre-a-tive power with you to share.

Words: Jann Aldredge-Clanton
Music: *Schlesische Volkslieder*, 1842

Words ©1996 Jann Aldredge-Clanton.

CRUSADERS' HYMN
Irregular

The Heavens Sing the Majesty
of All That Ruah* Made

Psalm 19:1-6

1. The heav-ens sing the maj-es-ty of all that Ru-ah made,
2. Great Ru-ah crowns all liv-ing ones with gifts so rich and rare,
3. Wise Ru-ah sends Her proph-ets out for lib-er-at-ing life,
4. Our hopes be-come re-al-i-ty as faith turns in-to sight;

While earth joins in with sym-pho-ny that sounds through hill and glade.
With o-ver-flow-ing nour-ish-ment for all to free-ly share.
For break-ing down op-pres-sion's wall, re-liev-ing pain and strife.
Re-joice and claim the vic-to-ry, a fu-ture free and bright;

A-wake, all peo-ple, near and far, Cre-a-tive Spir-it praise,
The moun-tains robed in roy-al-ty sur-round the o-ceans blue,
Re-lease all cap-tives ev-ery-where; fling wide the pris-on gates;
Come gath-er now in cir-cles wide; a-round the world join hands,

The One who dwells in ev-ery life, in-spir-ing all our days.
And fra-grant flow-ers clothe the fields in ev-ery shape and hue.
Come forth and wel-come lib-er-ty; our dream no long-er waits.
For sis-ter-hood and broth-er-hood u-nite to heal all lands.

*Hebrew word for "Spirit"

Words: Jann Aldredge-Clanton
Music: Samuel A. Ward

MATERNA
8.6.8.6.D.

Let All the Creation
Sing Forth with Elation

Genesis 1:1-2; Psalm 150:6; Isaiah 44:23, 55:12

1. Let all the cre - a - tion sing forth with e - la - tion To
2. The for - ests and o - ceans de - clare their de - vo - tion to

Ru - ah * the Spir - it, who gives birth to all. She nur - tures and
Ru - ah the Spir - it of Wis - dom and power. The trees clap their

feeds us, while gent - ly She leads us On path - ways of free - dom to
branch - es, and all heav - en danc - es; The breath of Great Ru - ah makes

fol - low our call. The moun - tains and riv - ers pro -
ev - ery - thing flower. All crea - tures a - dore Her and

claim Her the Giv - er Of beau - ty and bless - ings o'er -
gath - er be - fore Her, With prais - es that ring from the

*Hebrew word for "Spirit"

Words: Jann Aldredge-Clanton
Music: Welsh Melody

Words ©2000 Jann Aldredge-Clanton.

ASH GROVE
12.11.12.11.D

flow - ing each day. The don - keys and bea - gles, the mon - keys and
depths of the earth. As we join the sing - ing, our gifts glad - ly

ea - gles, All join Her cre - a - tive ex - u - ber - ant play.
bring - ing, We help Her to bring new cre - a - tion to birth.

80   Our Strong and Tender God We Praise

Psalm 138:2-3, 7

Descant

4. God's stead-fast love and faith-ful care Re - new our hearts each day.

Unison

1. Our strong and ten - der God we praise; She dwells with - in our souls,
2. And when we pass through trou-bled lands, No foe can bring a - larm.
3. God speaks to us with gen - tle voice; She hears us when we call.
4. God's stead - fast love and faith-ful care Re - new our hearts each day.

She gives us bold new dreams to dare, For - ev - er with us stays.

To strength-en us through - out our days, And make us ful - ly whole.
God stretch-es out Her might - y hands, And shel - ters us from harm.
Her com - fort makes our hearts re - joice; She is our all in all.
She gives us bold new dreams to dare, For - ev - er with us stays.

Words: Jann Aldredge-Clanton
Music: Larry E. Schultz

BLACK POINT CHURCH
8.6.8.6. (CM)

Our Strong and Tender God We Praise 80a

Psalm 138: 2-3, 7

1. Our strong and ten-der God we praise; She dwells with-in our souls,
2. And when we pass through trou-bled lands, No foe can bring a - larm.
3. God speaks to us with gen-tle voice; She hears us when we call.
4. God's stead-fast love and faith-ful care Re - new our hearts each day.

To strength-en us through-out our days, And make us ful-ly whole.
God stretch-es out Her might-y hands, And shel-ters us from harm.
Her com-fort makes our hearts re-joice; She is our all in all.
She gives us bold new dreams to dare, For - ev-er with us stays.

Words: Jann Aldredge-Clanton
Music: Carl G. Glaser
     Arr. Lowell Mason

AZMON
8.6.8.6. (CM)

81 New Miracles Unfold

Psalm 89:5; 2 Corinthians 5:17

1. New miracles unfold At dawn of every day,
2. The hills and valleys ring With Christ-Sophia's voice;
3. The sun in highest power Shines glory all around,
4. Join new creation's song Of Christ-Sophia's rise;

Fresh beauty to behold With sun's first shining ray.
Majestic birds take wing, As rocks and trees rejoice.
To bring all earth to flower, As heaven with praise resounds.
Come gladly sing along, And open wide all eyes.

A-wake and see, a-wake and see the whole world bloom with wonders free.

Words: Jann Aldredge-Clanton
Music: John Darwall

DARWALL
Irregular

Words ©1996 Jann Aldredge-Clanton.

Praise Our God, Eternal Goodness

82

Psalm 92:1-5

1. Praise our God, E - ter - nal Good - ness, Shin - ing bright - ly
2. Praise our God who gives us pow - er, For She dwells with -
3. Praise to God whose lov - ing kind - ness Flows forth free - ly

all a - round. Heaven and earth dis - play Her full - ness;
in us all. By Her grace we ful - ly flow - er,
all our days. Sing to Her a song of glad - ness,

With Her gifts we all a - bound. Al - le - lu - ia!
That we may ful - fill our call. Al - le - lu - ia!
For with us She ev - er stays. Al - le - lu - ia!

Al - le - lu - ia! Let us all God's prais - es sound.
Al - le - lu - ia! Look, She breaks down ev - ery wall.
Al - le - lu - ia! Look, She shows us Wis - dom's ways.

Words: Jann Aldredge-Clanton
Music: John Goss

LAUDA ANIMA
8.7.8.7.8.7

83

O Sister-Brother Spirit

Romans 8:14-15, 26-27; 1 Corinthians 12:8-11

1. O Sis - ter - Broth - er Spir - it, who dwells with-in us all,
2. O Sis - ter - Broth - er Spir - it, who deep with-in us sighs,
3. O Sis - ter - Broth - er Spir - it, who show - ers gifts on all,

In - spire us with your mis - sion, your lib - er - at - ing call.
We feel your strong com - pas - sion and hear your pain - ful cries;
Each one re - ceives your bless - ing and hears your gra - cious call.

Re - lease us from all bond - age and take a - way our fear;
We join your heal - ing la - bor for jus - tice and for peace;
We join your new cre - a - tion, un - fold - ing day by day;

O help us bring your free - dom to peo - ple far and near.
O fill us with your pow - er the cap - tives to re - lease.
O help us work to - geth - er to show your lov - ing way.

Words: Jann Aldredge-Clanton
Music: Arthur H. Mann

ANGEL'S STORY
7.6.7.6.D.

Our Mother Within Us

84

Isaiah 66:13; Psalm 144:9

1. Our Moth - er with - in us, so ho - ly and blessed,
2. Our Moth - er with - in us, so man - y your names,
3. O Moth - er with - in us, for - ev - er a - bide,

You nur - ture our spir - its with com - fort and rest.
Re - veal - ing our pow - er, you help us to claim
With bless - ings un - fold - ing and arms o - pen wide;

O give us your wis - dom and strength for each day,
Our voic - es of cour - age to speak a - gainst wrong,
You give us new vi - sions of life full and fair;

And fill us with love for all peo - ple, we pray.
And joy o - ver - flow - ing to sing a new song.
Your an - gels sur - round us with ten - der - est care.

Words: Jann Aldredge-Clanton
Music: James R. Murray

MUELLER
11.11.11.11.

85 Hope of Glory, Living in Us

Colossians 1:27; Romans 8:18-25; Proverbs 13:12

1. Hope of glo - ry, liv - ing in us, Christ - So - phi - a, you we praise.
2. Hope de - ferred makes hearts grow heav - y; Christ - So - phi - a, help us wait;
3. All cre - a - tion stands on tip - toe, long - ing toward re - veal - ing light;
4. Gra - cious, liv - ing hope of glo - ry, Christ - So - phi - a, you we bless;

By your name we gain fresh cour - age, strength to dare new trails to blaze.
Keep our vi - sions plain be - fore us, so re - solve will not a - bate.
Hope sus - tains the glo - rious mys - tery, till our faith turns in - to sight.
Voice of Wis - dom, deep with - in us, with your word our souls re - fresh.

May we feel your stir - ring Spir - it, lead - ing us as on we go;
Chal - lenged by your res - ur - rec - tion, we find hope to make things new;
Look, there springs a heal - ing riv - er, flow - ing by a tree of life;
Joy - ful res - ur - rec - tion sto - ry, mir - a - cle for all to claim,

Bring - ing change ful - fills our call - ing, though the way seems long and slow.
Now de - sire will find ful - fill - ment, as new life comes in - to view.
Quench - ing thirst for peace and jus - tice, all Earth's splen - dor to re - vive.
May we rise to full - est beau - ty by the pow - er of your name.

Words: Jann Aldredge-Clanton
Music: Rowland H. Prichard

HYFRYDOL
8.7.8.7.D.

Send Us Forth, O Christ-Sophia   86

Matthew 25:35-40; Matthew 5:13; Luke 13:20-21

1. Send us forth, O Christ-So-phi-a, on your mis-sion in your name;
2. May we see you, Christ-So-phi-a, all a-round us ev-ery-where,
3. For your mis-sion, Christ-So-phi-a, give us in-sight, hope and grace;
4. Christ-So-phi-a, You have called us, your great mis-sion to ful-fill;

Fill us with your lov-ing wis-dom, all your jus-tice to pro-claim.
In our sis-ters and our broth-ers hurt-ing for some-one to care.
May we see all liv-ing be-ings as re-flect-ing your bright face.
Grant us faith to go forth bold-ly, your just vi-sion to make real.

Help us change op-pres-sive sys-tems, lib-er-at-ing all with-in.
As we do for those who suf-fer, we do al-so un-to you,
Sis-ter Earth cries out in an-guish with all oth-ers last and least;
When our spir-its sag and fal-ter, give us hope to keep a-live,

Break-ing walls and build-ing bridg-es, right-ing wrongs, re-deem-ing sin.
Join-ing hands with one an-oth-er, we work to make all things new.
By re-stor-ing her rich beau-ty, we be-come the salt and yeast.
Cour-age to change words and ac-tions, all cre-a-tion to re-vive.

Words: Jann Aldredge-Clanton
Music: John Zundel

BEECHER
8.7.8.7.D.

Words ©1996 Jann Aldredge-Clanton.

We Claim Your Support, Christ-Sophia, Our Rock

1 Corinthians 10:4; Isaiah 51:1

1. We claim your sup - port, Christ - So - phi - a, our Rock;
2. O Rock of Cre - a - tion, from you we were made;
3. O Rock that is high - er than all of our dreams,
4. Cast out all our fears, Christ - So - phi - a, we pray;

Your life - giv - ing pow - ers our trea - sures un - lock.
We mir - ror your im - age which nev - er shall fade.
From depths of your beau - ty come free - flow - ing streams;
We call on your strength to cre - ate a new day.

Our tal - ents and grac - es re - store wea - ry land;
You nour - ish our gifts with your spir - i - tual flow;
We drink from your well of deep wis - dom and peace;
O Rock of Sal - va - tion, on you we de - pend;

O sol - id foun - da - tion, on you we can stand.
You strength - en our steps as new path - ways we show.
Your wa - ter of life brings cre - a - tive re - lease.
Your good - ness and kind - ness spring forth with - out end.

Words: Jann Aldredge-Clanton
Music: Joseph Funk's *Genuine Church Music*, 1832

Words ©1996 Jann Aldredge-Clanton.

FOUNDATION
11.11.11.11.

Come, Christ-Sophia, Our Way

88

Proverbs 4:11-18; John 14:6, 15:15

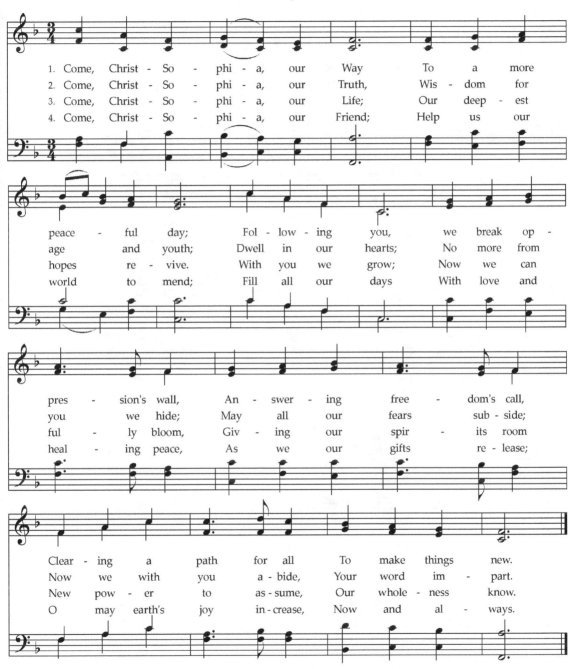

1. Come, Christ-So - phi - a, our Way To a more
2. Come, Christ-So - phi - a, our Truth, Wis - dom for
3. Come, Christ-So - phi - a, our Life; Our deep - est
4. Come, Christ-So - phi - a, our Friend; Help us our

peace - ful day; Fol - low - ing you, we break op -
age and youth; Dwell in our hearts; No more from
hopes re - vive. With you we grow; Now we can
world to mend; Fill all our days With love and

pres - sion's wall, An - swer - ing free - dom's call,
you we hide; May all our fears sub - side;
ful - ly bloom, Giv - ing our spir - its room
heal - ing peace, As we our gifts re - lease;

Clear - ing a path for all To make things new.
Now we with you a - bide, Your word im - part.
New pow - er to as - sume, Our whole - ness know.
O may earth's joy in - crease, Now and al - ways.

Words: Jann Aldredge-Clanton
Music: Felice de Giardini

ITALIAN HYMN
6.6.4.6.6.6.4.

Words ©1996 Jann Aldredge-Clanton.

89 Rise Up, O Christ-Sophia

John 14:6; Romans 8:19-23; Proverbs 3:13-15

1. Rise up, O Christ-So - phi - a, for you the whole world longs
2. Lead on, O Queen of Wis - dom; with you none can com - pare.
3. Guide us, thou Christ-So - phi - a, on paths of truth and light.

With ea - ger ex - pec - ta - tion, till you shall right our wrongs.
You are the truth with - in us; you shine through all that's fair.
Cre - a - tion yearns for free - dom in your pure beau - ty bright.

Your gen - tle words of wis - dom, your warm ca - ress of peace
Our hearts cry out for jus - tice midst con - flict, pain, and strife;
You call us as your min - is-ters, to serve with you on earth,

Em - pow - er us to la - bor with you our wars to cease.
You calm the rag - ing tem - pests to bring us peace and life.
To co - cre - ate a mys - tery, new life with you to birth.

Words: Jann Aldredge-Clanton
Music: Henry T. Smart

Words ©1996 Jann Aldredge-Clanton.

LANCASHIRE
7.6.7.6.D.

O Flower Blooming, Deep in Pain

Song of Songs 1:5-7; 2:1-2

1. O Flow-er bloom-ing, deep in pain,
2. Flow-er So-phi-a, rich in hue,
3. Rise from the dust of sa-cred page;
4. Lil-y So-phi-a, pure de-light,

Sti-fled, ne-glect-ed, cursed, and scorned;
Come-ly and dark, your im-age sur-vives;
In-to our world bloom fresh and free.
O Rose of Sha-ron, you in-spire

Lil-y of black, your beau-ty has lain
No e-vil force your power can sub-due;
Flow-er So-phi-a from age to age,
Cour-age to speak for truth and right,

Bur-ied in veils, passed by, for-lorn.
Though oft cast down your Spir-it thrives.
O-pen our eyes your full-ness to see.
Faith to ful-fill our soul's de-sire.

Words: Jann Aldredge-Clanton
Music: Lowell Mason

Words ©1996 Jann Aldredge-Clanton.

HAMBURG
8.8.8.8. (LM)

91 Go Forth, O Christ-Sophia

Ephesians 2:14-15, 19

1. Go forth, O Christ-Sophia, to make our world a-new;
2. Help us, O Christ-Sophia, to break down dogma's wall,
3. In-spire us, Christ-Sophia, to do your work of peace,

O may we join your mis-sion and show your wid-er view.
So all are free to fol-low the Ho-ly Spir-it's call.
That jus-tice will flow free-ly, and all our wars will cease.

We will not fear nor fal-ter though storms rage all a-round;
No creed nor rule can sti-fle our voic-es clear and strong,
U-nit-ed we move for-ward to o-pen ev-ery door,

For you are with us al-ways; your strength in us a-bounds.
For we are build-ing bridg-es and o-ver-com-ing wrong.
So all are ful-ly wel-comed and blessed for-ev-er-more.

Words: Jann Aldredge-Clanton
Music: George J. Webb

WEBB
7.6.7.6.D.

Midwife Divine Now Calls Us

92

Psalm 22:9-10

1. Mid - wife Di - vine now calls us forth from our safe - est place,
2. Mid - wife Di - vine in - spires us through ho - ly dark - ness deep,
3. O may we join Her la - bor to bring new life to birth;

Beck - on - ing al - ways for - ward out in - to un - known space.
Mov - ing through realms of mys - tery to wake all dreams that sleep.
Crowned in Her an - cient splen - dor, we claim our sa - cred worth.

She sings a birth - ing song To calm our
Her lov - ing plan un - folds As ten - der -
Our Mid - wife shows the way To worlds of

fears and help us Through days so hard and long.
ly She guides us Through path - ways new and bold.
love and beau - ty, More than our words can say.

Words: Jann Aldredge-Clanton
Music: *Geistliche Kirchengesang*, 1599
Harm. by Michael Praetorious

ES IST EIN ROS'
Irregular

Words ©1999 Jann Aldredge-Clanton.

93

O Come, Christ-Sophia

1 Corinthians 1:24; Psalm 96:1

Words: Jann Aldredge-Clanton
Music: John Francis Wade

ADESTE FIDELES
Irregular with Refrain

Sophia, Wisdom Deep in Our Souls   94

Proverbs 3:13-18; 8:7-11

1. So - phi - a, Wis - dom deep in our souls, Brings bless-ings more
2. So - phi - a, Wis - dom, brings us new life, Bloom-ing in our
3. So - phi - a, Wis - dom, sounds Her clear call To join Her cre -

pre - cious than sil - ver or gold. She guides our steps on
hearts to end all strife. She helps us stand for
a - tion of beau - ty for all. She leads the way to

path-ways of peace, And fills us with pow - er our gifts to in - crease.
jus - tice and right, And o - pens the doors to our dreams day and night.
trea-sures so rare, And gives us the cour-age new ven - tures to dare.

So - phi - a Friend, So - phi - a Friend, Comes with Her grace our world to mend.

Words: Jann Aldredge-Clanton
Music: Traditional English Carol

THE FIRST NOWELL
Irregular

95 Christ-Sophia Now We Welcome

1 Corinthians 1:24-30; Colossians 1:27; 2 Timothy 1:7

1. Christ-So-phi-a now we wel-come, Hope for peo-ple ev-ery-where,
2. Christ-So-phi-a gives us pow-er To trans-form our world to-day;
3. Christ-So-phi-a, hope of glo-ry, Well of Wis-dom in our souls,

Born to bring us full-est free-dom, Call-ing us to dream and dare.
Love and grace on all we show-er, Help-ing make a peace-ful way.
Stirs us to re-claim the sto-ry Of cre-a-tion blessed and whole.

Come, re-joic-ing; come, re-joic-ing; Christ-So-phi-a sets us free.
Come, re-joic-ing; come, re-joic-ing; Christ-So-phi-a sets us free.
Come, re-joic-ing; come, re-joic-ing; Christ-So-phi-a sets us free.

Words: Jann Aldredge-Clanton
Music: Henry T. Smart

REGENT SQUARE
8.7.8.7.8.7.

Words ©2000 Jann Aldredge-Clanton.

Christ-Sophia Now We Praise

96

Proverbs 8:23-35; John 14:6

1. Christ-So-phi-a now we praise; Joy-ful songs our voic-es raise,
2. Praise the glo-rious Queen of Wis-dom; Praise the Ev-er-last-ing One.
3. Christ-So-phi-a is the way, truth, and life for us to-day.

For new life in us to birth, For deep heal-ing of the earth.
Life and hope to all She brings; Pris-on doors wide o-pen flings.
By Her Spir-it in us all, We take up the jus-tice call.

Long Her face we did not see; Blind no more our eyes shall be;
Lib-er-ty is ours to claim By the pow-er of Her name.
Fear not, She will give us cour-age To make peace, all be-ings nour-ish.

Long we've need-ed Her em-brace, Glo-ry and pow-er of Her grace.
Shout for joy; sound free-dom's cry; All na-ture sing, for She is nigh.
Come, join hands; let us u-nite, Walk-ing to-geth-er in-to light.

Christ-So-phi-a now we praise; Joy-ful songs our voic-es raise.

Words: Jann Aldredge-Clanton
Music: Felix Mendelssohn
arr. William H. Cummings

Words ©1996 Jann Aldredge-Clanton.

MENDELSSOHN
7.7.7.7.D. with Refrain

97 O Christ-Sophia, Be Born in Us

Isaiah 9:2-4, Luke 1:52-53, 2:10-14

1. O Christ-Sophia, be born in us, we need your power and grace;
2. O Christ-Sophia, your radiant life shines through the winter's night.
3. O Christ-Sophia, come dwell in us, for you our spirits long;

En-cour-age us to la-bor long in-jus-tice to e-rase.
Your ten-der touch re-stores our souls and brings new truth to sight.
In-spire our dreams and stir our hopes with bless-ed an-gel's song:

Come, help us break op-pres-sion's yoke and end the bit-ter strife;
A-wak-en us to change our world, your im-age ful-ly show,
"Fear not, be-hold the peace-ful land where dawns a glo-rious morn;

Lift up the low-ly, poor, and weak to fresh, a-bun-dant life.
All wom-en, men, and chil-dren free to love, cre-ate, and grow.
Good news of joy to all the earth, for Christ-So-phi-a is born."

Words: Jann Aldredge-Clanton
Music: Richard Storrs Willis

Words ©1996 Jann Aldredge-Clanton.

CAROL
8.6.8.6.D. (CMD)

Sound Forth the News That Wisdom Comes

Proverbs 3:17-18; 4:8-9

1. Sound forth the news that Wis-dom comes To bring new life to birth.
2. No more let fear and cus-tom hide The path of Wis-dom fair.
3. Joy-ful are we who heed the call Of Wis-dom in our souls.
4. Crown Wis-dom Queen of heaven and earth. Her reign will set us free.

A-rise with hope, Her la-bor join,
She leads the way to life and joy,
With Her we break op-pres-sion's wall,
Fling wide the gates that all may come

And peace shall fill the earth, And peace shall fill the
With gifts for all to share, With gifts for all to
So love may free-ly flow, So love may free-ly
Join hands and dance with glee, Join hands and dance with

1. And peace shall fill the earth,

1. And peace shall fill the earth, And

earth, And peace, and peace shall fill the earth.
share, With gifts, with gifts for all to share.
flow, So love, so love may free-ly flow.
glee, Join hands, join hands and dance with glee.

peace shall fill the earth,

Words: Jann Aldredge-Clanton
Music: George Frederick Handel   Arr. by Lowell Mason   Words ©2001 Jann Aldredge-Clanton.

ANTIOCH
Irregular

99 O Holy Darkness, Loving Womb

Psalm 139:12; Isaiah 45:3

1. O Ho-ly Dark-ness, lov-ing womb, who nur-tures and cre-ates,
2. Cre-a-tive Dark-ness, clos-est friend, you whis-per in the night;
3. O Ho-ly Night of deep-est bliss, we cel-e-brate your power;
4. O Ho-ly Christ-So-phi-a, your im-age, black and fair,

Sus-tain us through the long-est night with dreams of o-pen gates.
You calm our fears as un-known paths sur-prise us with new sight.
In-fuse us with your en-er-gy that brings our seeds to flower.
Stirs us to end in-jus-tice and the wounds of Earth re-pair.

We move in-side to mys-ter-y that in our cen-ter dwells,
We mar-vel at your boun-ty, your gifts so full and free,
The voice out of the dark-ness ex-cites our warm-est zeal
The trea-sures of your dark-ness and rich-es of your grace

Where streams of rich-est beau-ty flow from sa-cred liv-ing wells.
Un-fold-ing as you wak-en us to new re-al-i-ty.
To bring to-geth-er dark and light, true ho-li-ness re-veal.
In-spire us to ful-fill our call, our sa-cred-ness em-brace.

Words: Jann Aldredge-Clanton
Music: Lewis H. Redner

Words ©1996 Jann Aldredge-Clanton.

ST. LOUIS
Irregular

What Wondrous Thing

100

Jeremiah 31:22

1. What won-drous thing is happen-ing here Where minds and souls are open-ing?
2. A new thing springs forth on the earth, With bless-ing, hope, and heal-ing;
3. E - piph-a - ny sur - rounds us now, As we re - claim our whole-ness;

The scales fall off our blind - ed eyes; New sight a - rous - es hop-ing.
The power of wom - an saves all life, So - phi - a - Christ re - veal-ing.
So - phi - a - Christ with - in us all, In - spires us with new bold-ness.

Look, look, for She is here; Her wis - dom words have long been near.

Now, now, be - hold Her grace, Di - vin - i - ty in Her im - age.

Words: Jann Aldredge-Clanton
Music: Traditional English Melody, 16th C.
Harm. John Stainer

GREENSLEEVES
8.7.8.7. with Refrain

If This Is the Fast
(Then Our Light Shall Break Forth)

Isaiah 58:6-8a

Cantor: If this is the fast we would choose: to loose the bonds, to
this is the fast we would choose: to share our bread, to

break the yoke, to let the op-pressed go free, Then our
clothe the poor, to hide not our-selves from our own,

[upward gliss. on chime tree]

light shall break forth like the dawn, **Cantor:** and our

Congregation: Then our light shall break forth like the dawn,

heal-ing shall spring forth quick-ly! **Cantor:** If

Congregation: and our heal-ing shall spring forth quick-ly!

Words: Isaiah 58:6-8a; Larry E. Schultz
Music: Larry E. Schultz

J. MCKINNEY
Irregular

Cantor: Then our light shall break forth like the dawn,

quick-ly!

Congregation: Then our light shall break forth like the

f [improvised up and down gliss.
on chime tree through M. 25]

Cantor: and our heal-ing shall spring forth quick-ly!

dawn,

Congregation: and our heal-ing shall spring forth

[chime tree fades out]

freely
mp *molto. rit*

Cantor: If this is the fast we would choose.

quick-ly!

mp *freely*
molto. rit

102 O Mother Rock Who Bore Us

Deuteronomy 32:18

1. O Moth-er Rock who bore us, un-mind-ful we have been
2. Our world cries out in an-guish from our ne-glect of you;
3. Teach us to be more mind-ful, O Rock who gave us birth,

Of all your good-ness to us, your mer-cy with-out end.
O Moth-er Rock who bore us, come now our souls re-new.
Re-flect-ing on your beau-ty that per-me-ates the earth.

We've praised our Fa-ther ful-ly, but scorned your im-age fair,
For-give our long for-get-ting of your strong lov-ing care;
Re-store our child-like won-der, as we up-on you gaze,

Re-ject-ing all your wis-dom that shines forth ev-ery-where.
O may we now dis-cov-er your gifts for all to share.
And may we give you glad-ly our songs of end-less praise.

Words: Jann Aldredge-Clanton
Music: Hans Leo Hassler   Harm. Johann Sebastian Bach   Words ©1996 Jann Aldredge-Clanton.

PASSION CHORALE
7.6.7.6.D.

Do You Want to Be Healed?

103

John 5:2-9

1. "Do you want to be healed?" calls a voice ten-der-ly; "Do
2. "Rise up, em-brace new life," calls the voice ur-gent-ly; "New
3. We hear your voice with-in, call-ing us, call-ing us; O

you want to be healed and made well? If you want to be whole, Cast
life is wait-ing for your em-brace. Take up your free-dom now; Your
Christ-So-phi-a, we hear your voice. Help us to claim your grace, Old

off each crip-pling role; Un-chain your fet-tered soul; be set
spir-it's growth al-low; Move for-ward in-to your full-est
pat-terns to e-rase; Your new cre-a-tion's sign, we will

free; be set free; Un-chain your fet-tered soul; be set free."
wis-dom and health; Move for-ward in-to your full-est self."
be; we will be; Your new cre-a-tion's sign, we will be.

Words: Jann Aldredge-Clanton
Music: William Walker's *Southern Harmony*, 1835

WONDROUS LOVE
Irregular

104 O Blessed Christ-Sophia

Isaiah 53:3; John 12:12-16

1. O bless-ed Christ-So-phi - a, to you we lift our praise;
2. You en-ter hum-ble set - tings and grace com-mu-ni - ties;
3. Now make tri-um-phal en - try in - to our minds and souls;
4. Most Ho-ly Christ-So-phi - a, O wise and bless-ed one,

In grate-ful ad - o - ra - tion, our voic - es now we raise.
Re-ceive a roy - al wel - come from ev - ery-one who sees.
O bless-ed Christ-So - phi - a, in - spire our dreams and goals.
To you we sing ho - san - nas; your vic - to - ry is won.

Too long your name and im - age we've hid-den from our eyes;
O bless-ed Christ-So - phi - a, you come in ev - ery age,
O may we catch your vi - sion of part-ner-ship and peace,
The palm trees wave their branch - es to cel - e - brate your reign;

Too long your words of wis - dom, re - ject-ed and de - spised.
Un - set-tling priest and proph - et, sur - pris-ing wis - est sage.
Trans-form-ing all our la - bor, our tal - ents to re - lease.
We dance in ex - pec - ta - ion of whole-ness to re - gain.

Words: Jann Aldredge-Clanton
Music: Melchior Teschner

ST. THEODULPH
Irregular

Words ©1996 Jann Aldredge-Clanton.

Christ-Sophia Lives Today

105

Matthew 28:1-10; John 14:6; Habakkuk 2:2-3

1. Christ-So-phi-a lives to-day, Al - - le - lu - ia!
2. Sing we now this bless-ed morn, Al - - le - lu - ia!
3. Cel-e-brate a bright new life, Al - - le - lu - ia!
4. Christ-So-phi-a ris-es glo-rious, Al - - le - lu - ia!

Show-ing us the truth, the way, Al - - le - lu - ia!
Christ-So-phi-a's work is born, Al - - le - lu - ia!
Christ-So-phi-a ends the strife, Al - - le - lu - ia!
All cre-a-tion sings vic-to-rious, Al - - le - lu - ia!

Free at last, we all can be, Al - - le - lu - ia!
Wis-dom, jus-tice, lib-er-ty, Al - - le - lu - ia!
Sound the news to ev-ery land, Al - - le - lu - ia!
Hope springs forth; sur-prise a-bounds, Al - - le - lu - ia!

Make the vi-sion plain to see, Al - - le - lu - ia!
Come, cre-ate the ju-bi-lee, Al - - le - lu - ia!
Join to-geth-er, hand in hand, Al - - le - lu - ia!
Earth trans-formed with joy re-sounds, Al - - le - lu - ia!

Words: Jann Aldredge-Clanton
Music: *Lyra Davidica*, 1708

Words ©1996 Jann Aldredge-Clanton.

EASTER HYMN
7.7.7.7. with Alleluias

106 Up from the Grave

Proverbs 1:20-23; 3:16-18

1. Bu - ried and scoffed She lay, Wis-dom, So - phi - a; Cry - ing to show the way,
2. Long has She suf - fered scorn, Wis-dom, So - phi - a; Now is Her truth re - born,
3. No force could keep Her bound, Wis-dom, So - phi - a; Glo - rious new life She found,

Wis - dom and Friend. Up from the grave She a - rose, With a

She a - rose,

might - y tri - umph o'er Her foes; She a - rose a vic - tor o - ver

She a - rose!

death and pain, And She lives for - ev - er with us all to reign.

She a - rose! She a - rose! Praise So - phi - a, She a - rose!

She a - rose! She a - rose!

Words: Jann Aldredge-Clanton
Music: Robert Lowry

Words ©2002 Jann Aldredge-Clanton.

CHRIST AROSE
Irregular

O Holy Spirit, Come Dwell in Our Souls 107

Acts 2:17-18; Isaiah 11:6

1. O Ho-ly Spir-it, come dwell in our souls,
2. O Spir-it, fill our world with life a-new,
3. Spir-it, your lov-ing power brings truth and right;

That we may know your truth that makes us whole.
That old and young may see your full-er view.
Both men and wom-en preach new vi-sions bright.

We praise your sa-cred gifts, poured out on all,
Then shall the walls come down, all shall be free,
Chil-dren shall lead the way, dream-ing new dreams,

Daugh-ters and sons shall preach your free-dom's call.
And we can grow to be all we can be.
And all shall live in peace be-side clear streams.

Words: Jann Aldredge-Clanton
Music: William F. Sherwin

BREAD OF LIFE
6.4.6.4.D.

108 Come, Holy Spirit, to Change Us

Acts 2:1-20

1. Come, Ho-ly Spir-it, to change us, Hold-ing new life in your hands;
2. Sis-ters and broth-ers to-geth-er Preach the Good News of your grace,
3. Vi-sions of splen-dor sur-round us, Beck-on-ing for-ward each day;

Come, Ho-ly Spir-it, to bless us, Show-ing the way to new lands.
Spread-ing your love through all na-tions, Work-ing to free ev-ery race.
Dreams of our sons and our daugh-ters Lead in cre-at-ing new ways.

Come, Ho-ly Spir-it, Show-er-ing gifts on us all;

Wom-en and men feel your pow-er, Join-ing to fol-low your call.

Words: Jann Aldredge-Clanton
Music: James McGranahan

SHOWERS OF BLESSING
8.7.8.7. with Refrain

We Gather with Hope
and a Vision of Peace

Acts 2:1-20

1. We gath-er with hope and a vi-sion of peace;
2. We o-pen our hearts to a still wid-er view,
3. All rac-es join hands, and to-geth-er we pray;

With hearts full of long-ing our prayers nev-er cease.
As wom-en and men join to preach the Good News.
Our sons and our daugh-ters pro-claim a new way.

Like the sound of rush-ing wind-storms and the blaze of the fire,

Comes the pow-er of the Spir-it, our dreams to in-spire.

Words: Jann Aldredge-Clanton
Music: John J. Husband

REVIVE US AGAIN
11.11. with Refrain

Come and Feast,
for All Are Welcomed

Matthew 26:6-13, 26-29

Descant

4. With the Spir-it-blessed com-mis-sion, "Go and serve this meal to all,"

* 1. Come and feast, for all are wel-comed at God's ta-ble spread with love.
2. Here we nur-ture and en-cour-age as we share this com-mon meal,
3. See the chal-ice lift-ed up-ward; smell the fra-grant, bro-ken bread;
4. With the Spir-it-blessed com-mis-sion, "Go and serve this meal to all,"

take its love and peace-ful vi-sion in-to ev-ery ban-quet hall.

Come pro-claim God's grace and good-ness in, a-round us, and a-bove.
while we fos-ter deep com-mu-nion and our in-ner-selves re-veal.
taste the gifts from field and vine-yard; hear the words that Je-sus said:
take its love and peace-ful vi-sion in-to ev-ery ban-quet hall.

Go and serve as nour-ished peo-ple, glad-ly feed-ing one and all!

Come and feast, for all are wel-comed at God's ta-ble spread with love.
Here we nur-ture and en-cour-age as we share this com-mon meal.
"Eat and drink, and in re-mem-brance touch your souls with wine and bread."
Go and serve as nour-ished peo-ple, glad-ly feed-ing one and all!

*Stanzas 1-3 may be sung prior to communion as a Call to the Table.
Stanza 4 may be offered as a Sending Forth.

Words: Larry E. Schultz
Music: Henry T. Smart
Descant by Larry E. Schultz

REGENT SQUARE
8.7.8.7.8.7.

We Invite All to Join Our Circle Wide **111**

Ephesians 3:16-19

1. We in-vite all to join our cir-cle wide;
2. Come and find heal-ing in our cir-cle wide;
3. May our cir-cle keep grow-ing deep and wide;

We in-vite all to join our cir-cle wide.
Come and find heal-ing in our cir-cle wide.
May our cir-cle keep grow-ing deep and wide.

With our arms o-pen wide, We will join in a feast of love,

With Christ - So - phi - a be - side.

Words: Jann Aldredge-Clanton
Music: African-American Spiritual

BREAK BREAD
Irregular

Words ©2000 Jann Aldredge-Clanton.

112

Come, Thou from Whom All Blessings Flow

Proverbs 3:17; Revelation 21:5

1. Come, Thou from whom all bless-ings flow; Wake us to see more than we know. Help us claim all our gifts and power. Fill us with grace that we may flower.

2. Come, Giv-er of all life and peace; May we join you in Earth's in-crease. Grant us new cour-age for this day That we may find true Wis-dom's way.

3. Come, Spir-it who makes all things new; Show us your wid-er, full-er view. Teach us our whole-ness now to see; Stir us to be all we can be.

Words: Jann Aldredge-Clanton
Music: Louis Bourgeois

OLD 100TH
8.8.8.8. (LM)

Arise, My Love

113

Song of Songs 2:10-13

1. A - rise, my love, my fair one, come; For now the win - ter-
2. Cre - a - tion's mu - sic has be - gun; The time for sing - ing
3. The fig tree bears its rip - ened fruit; The fra - grant vines per -

time is past. The rain is o - ver and is gone.
is at hand. The coo - ing of the tur - tle - dove
fume the day. A - rise my love, my fair one, come;

The flowers ap - pear on earth at last.
Is gent - ly heard through - out the land.
A - rise, my love, and come a - way.

Words: Song of Songs 2:10-13; Larry E. Schultz
Music: Larry E. Schultz

CINDY'S SONG
8.8.8.8. (LM)

113a

Arise, My Love

Song of Songs 2:10-13

1. A - rise, my love, my fair one, come; For now the win - ter time is past. The rain is o - ver and is gone. The flowers ap - pear on earth at last.
2. Cre - a - tion's mu - sic has be - gun; The time for sing - ing is at hand. The coo - ing of the tur - tle - dove Is gent - ly heard through - out the land.
3. The fig tree bears its rip - ened fruit; The fra - grant vines per - fume the day. A - rise, my love, my fair one come; A - rise my love and come a - way.

Words: Song of Songs 2:10-13; Larry E. Schultz
Music: Robert Schumann

CANONBURY
8.8.8.8. (LM)

Christ-Sophia Now We Bless

Psalm 104

1. Christ - So-phi - a   now   we   bless;   Songs   of   joy   our   thanks pro - fess.
2. Christ - So-phi - a   comes in   light,   Touch - ing earth with   beau - ty bright;
3. Christ - So-phi - a   fills   the   earth   With   a - bun - dant   love   and mirth.
4. Christ - So-phi - a   stirs   our hearts   With   a   vi - sion   to   im - part,

We   re - joice   in   ev - ery grace,   Beau - ty   glow - ing   in   each   face,
Val - leys gush forth   crys - tal streams;   Rock - y   can - yons   blush with dreams;
Char - iot clouds on   an - gel wings,   Glad - ness   to   all   hearts they bring.
All   cre - a - tion   fed   and full,   Freed from   ev - ery   sti - fling   rule,

Fra - grant flowers and   gold - en grain,   Sing - ing   birds,   re - fresh - ing   rain;
Graz - ing   cat - tle,   moun-tain goats,   Friend - ly squirrels and   spright - ly colts,
Car - ing   friends who   gath - er   near   Share   our   laugh - ter,   hopes, and tears.
Men   and   wom - en   shar - ing power,   Part - ners   for   all   gifts   to flower.

All   these gifts   our   souls in - spire,   Light - ing   our   cre -   a - tive fire.
Liv - ing   be - ings   great   and small,   Wis - dom made   and   keeps them all.
For   these gifts   so   rich and free,   May   we   ev - er   grate - ful   be.
For   this world   our   spir - its pray;   Christ - So - phi - a   lights the way.

Words: Jann Aldredge-Clanton
Music: George J. Elvey

ST. GEORGE'S WINDSOR
7.7.7.7.D.

115   We Give Thanks to You, Dear Earth

Proverbs 4:11; 6:6-8

1. We give thanks to you, dear Earth, For your gifts so rich and rare,
2. Love-ly Earth, your glo-ry fills Laugh-ing brooks and flower-ing trees,
3. All your life deep val-ue holds; Small-est ants teach Wis-dom's way;
4. Hear, O Earth, our sol-emn vow To con-serve your sa-cred life,

For new life you bring to birth, Teach-ing us your ten-der care.
Soar-ing birds o'er gold-en hills, Danc-ing deer so wild and free.
Work-ing hard they share all loads, E-qual part-ners ev-ery day.
Car-ing for your fu-ture now, So your won-ders will sur-vive.

May we nur-ture you each day; Christ-So-phi-a guides our way.
May we nur-ture you each day; Christ-So-phi-a guides our way.
May we join them as we say, "Christ So-phi-a guides our way."
May we nur-ture you each day; Christ-So-phi-a guides our way.

Words: Jann Aldredge-Clanton
Music: Conrad Kocher
     adapt. William Henry Monk

DIX
7.7.7.7.7.7.

We Sound a Call to Freedom

116

Isaiah 58:6-8; John 8:32

1. We sound a call to free-dom that will heal our bro-ken land; As the
2. We are tired of i-dle prom-is-es and to-ken words and deeds; We want
3. Our re-cov-er-y is com-ing as our eyes re-ceive new sight; We are
* 4. Now our joy breaks forth in dawn-ing of a free and glo-rious day, And our

call rings out more clear-ly, vio-lent forc-es will dis-band. Pris-on
e-qual rights and ben-e-fits for ev-ery race and creed. Cries of
mov-ing out of bond-age; we are bound for free-dom bright. As we
heal-ing springs up quick-ly as our tal-ents we dis-play. Come and

doors will o-pen; bonds will loos-en by the Spir-it's hand; The truth will set us free.
wom-en, men, and chil-dren we want ev-ery-one to heed; The truth will set us free.
claim our full-est pow-ers, we walk on in-to the light; The truth will set us free.
join our cel-e-bra-tion; come re-joice and glad-ly say: The truth has set us free.

Free at last, O Hal-le-lu-jah! Free at last, O Hal-le-lu-jah!

Christ-So-phi-a, you have freed us! Your truth has set us free.

*Begin stanza 4 slowly and softly, gradually increasing in speed and volume.

Words: Jann Aldredge-Clanton
Music: American Folk Song, 19th C.

BATTLE HYMN
Irregular

Words ©1996 Jann Aldredge-Clanton.

NOTES

1. **Sister Spirit, Brother Spirit**
18. **O Spirit of Power**

These two hymns were among the first in my collaboration with Larry Schultz. SPIRIT DANCE was composed for "Sister Spirit, Brother Spirit" to celebrate the installation of Nancy Petty and Jack McKinney as co-pastors of Pullen Memorial Baptist Church. SOARING SONG was composed for "O Spirit of Power." Larry named this tune from a line in the hymn, "Cast out all our fear so with you we can soar," and from "Mother Eagle" God-imagery in several of my texts. Both these hymns have been sung, with orchestra, handbell, piano, and organ accompaniment, at Pentecost celebrations at Pullen. Larry and I believe that Sister-Brother Spirit brought us together as collaborators. From this collaboration also has come *Imagine God! A Children's Musical Exploring and Expressing Images of God* (Choristers Guild, 2004), other hymns in this collection, and "We Thank You, God, for Animal Friends," a children's anthem to be published by Choristers Guild in 2007. Larry and I presented a sectional entitled "Finding New Images for God," at the 2002 annual meeting of The Hymn Society.

1a. **Sister Spirit, Brother Spirit**
18a. **O Spirit of Power**

These hymns were sung at the 2001 Alliance of Baptists Annual Convocation, held at Oakhurst Baptist Church in Atlanta, Georgia. At the Convocation I gave a covenant address entitled "A Still More Excellent Way in Worship," emphasizing the ways in which inclusive divine images contribute to justice and peace. Several months later, Larry E. Schultz (who had been at the Alliance of Baptists Convocation) wrote me, requesting permission to use these two hymns in a worship service at Pullen Memorial Baptist Church in Raleigh, North Carolina, where he served as minister of music.

19.   Welcome Our Sister-Brother Creator
45.   Come, Sister-Brother Spirit

These two hymns and others in this collection pair Sister and Brother images to connote partnership in human relationships and opportunities for partnership with the Divine. Sister-Brother Divine images suggest mutuality more than do parental images. The Sister images in these hymns also celebrate my sister, Anne, an inspiring and encouraging partner who seeks to open people's minds to "fuller, wider views." The Brother images also celebrate my sons, Chad and Brett, whose strong brotherly love contributes to the "new creation."

22.   Our God Is a Mother and a Father

This hymn text affirms that God's image is in every person, but is also so much more. The arrangement of the Shaker tune, SIMPLE GIFTS, by Larry Schultz is derived from the arrangement in the musical, *Imagine God!* (Choristers Guild, 2004), by Larry and me. The musical's Production Guide offers instructions for a circle dance which can accompany the singing of the hymn. *Imagine God!* resources are available from Choristers Guild (each sold separately): Score (CGC48); Demo CD (CGCD11); Accompaniment CD (CGCD12); Preview Kit [contains score/demo CD] (CGK24); Production Guide (CGBK65) (www.choristers.guild.org).

47.   Father-Mother, Kind and Loving
74.   O Mother-Father God

These hymns and others in this collection pair Father and Mother images to describe God, who includes the best qualities associated with both fathers and mothers. To counter traditional stereotyping of feminine and masculine traits, these hymns image both Father and Mother as gentle and strong, nurturing and creative. The images in these hymns also describe my mother and father: their nurturing care, their "kind and loving" support, and their creativity. In addition, the images reflect the "strong and tender care" of my husband, David, for our sons.

57.   Welcome New Wineskins

This hymn and many others in *Inclusive Hymns for Liberating Christians* are inspired by an inclusive worship community called "New Wineskins." The name of this community comes from the metaphor in Matthew 9:17, describing our search for new language and symbols to proclaim the Gospel of liberation and shalom. The community's worship includes feminine and masculine divine names to support the "new peace and freedom" we sing and celebrate. In Dallas, Texas, CityChurch, Grace United Methodist Church, and Cathedral of Hope have welcomed New Wineskins and invited the community to lead their worship. These worship services included some of the hymns in this collection. New Wineskins Community has encouraged me in the creation of these hymns, and has sung them in the worship services of the Community. Hymns in this collection have also been included in worship services at Perkins School of Theology and Royal Lane Baptist Church, Dallas. In addition, they have been sung at an International Peace Conference, Cooperative Baptist Fellowship annual meetings, Central Texas United Methodist Fall University, Alliance of Baptists Annual Convocation, Perkins School of Theology Women's Week Conference, a Disciples of Christ School of Theology for the Laity, a conference sponsored by Highland Park United Methodist Church of Dallas and Perkins School of Theology, a conference sponsored by Unity Church of Dallas, clergy-women's groups, church Bible study groups, and church retreats.

58.   Creator God of Many Names

This hymn summarizes the theology at the foundation of *Inclusive Hymns for Liberating Christians*. The infinite Creator of the universe exceeds all our thoughts and words. All our language for divinity is metaphorical. A wide variety of divine names and images suggests the vastness and all-inclusiveness of our Creator. An inclusive image of the Creator contributes to a belief that all people are created in the divine image and thus have sacred value. Peace and "justice for each race" flow from this belief. The fresh, vibrant tune Larry Schultz composed for this hymn enhances the meaning. The music inspires openness to the Creator's "widest view" and the Spirit's "visions bright and new."

Larry honored me by naming the tune ALDREDGE-CLANTON, in gratitude for our creative collaborations.

61.   Are You Good and Are You Strong?

This hymn began the collaboration of composer Larry E. Schultz and me. Shortly after I gave permission for Pullen Memorial Baptist to use "Sister Spirit, Brother Spirit" (1a) and "O Spirit of Power" (18a), Larry wrote me, asking if I had any texts without music. Before this, I had been writing hymn texts to familiar hymn tunes, with one exception. I emailed Larry this text with a suggested melody line. On the morning of September 11, 2001, Larry opened this email and found the text "Are You Good and Are You Strong?" Larry said it was a cathartic experience for him to take this text and melody, and compose a hymn tune and children's anthem. The text seeks to express theodicy struggles. Can God be all good and all-powerful with so much suffering and evil in the world? Thus the hymn tune is named THEODICY. The hymn text is in the form of a child's questions. The last music phrase mimics the pitches from what musicologists call the "international children's chant," a series of notes (Sol-Mi-La-Sol-Mi) recognized and naturally sung by children all over the world.

62. God Like a Mother Comes Tenderly Near

This hymn is based on two of my favorite biblical images of God as Mother. As a hospital chaplain, I often use the comforting image from Isaiah 66:13: "As a mother comforts her child, so I will comfort you."

73. A Living Celebration of Christ's Love

Illuminating the functions of the Church, this hymn is based on the mission statement of First Baptist Church, Greenwood, South Carolina. Larry Schultz wrote the text and tune for the hymn to celebrate this congregation's 120th anniversary. The tune GRACE STREET is named for the street on which the church exists.

80. Our Strong and Tender God We Praise

Larry Schultz originally wrote this tune with a specific text in 2003 as an entry in a hymn contest celebrating the 275th anniversary of First Congregational Church, Scarborough, Maine. BLACK POINT CHURCH, the hymn tune, is an historic name for this church. This tune and text won the church's hymn competition. Larry suggested this tune for my text "Our Strong and Tender God We Praise." This tune supports the "strong" and "tender" divine images in the text. The descant on the final stanza can make this hymn especially stirring.

93. O Come, Christ-Sophia
96. Christ-Sophia Now We Praise

These are the first two hymns I wrote. It was in the Advent season of 1994, when I was seeking to give liturgical application to the inclusive Christology elaborated in my book *In Search of the Christ-Sophia: An Inclusive Christology for Liberating Christians* (Twenty-Third Publications, 1995; Eakin Press, 2004). I had become especially aware of the exclusively masculine language in traditional

Christmas carols, so I wrote "O Come, Christ-Sophia" and "Christ-Sophia Now We Praise" with gender-balanced Christological imagery. These two hymns were subsequently published in *Praying with Christ-Sophia: Services for Healing and Renewal* (Twenty-Third Publications, 1996), along with 34 other hymns that are also included in *Inclusive Hymns for Liberating Christians* (numbers 10, 11, 12, 19, 26, 35, 36, 37, 44, 49, 52, 68, 69, 70, 76, 77, 81, 85, 86, 87, 88, 89, 90, 97, 99, 100, 102, 103, 104, 105, 112, 114, 115, 116). Many of these hymns focus on Christ-Sophia, a symbol drawn from the biblical parallel between Jesus Christ and Wisdom (*Sophia* in the Greek language of the Christian Scriptures). These books on Christ-Sophia and books on other inclusive divine images are also available on www.jannaldredgeclanton.com.

101.   If This Is the Fast (Then Our Light Shall Break Forth)

Larry Schultz wrote this text, closely based on Isaiah 58: 6-8a, and tune for the 2006 Ash Wednesday service at Pullen Memorial Baptist Church. The tune name, J. MCKINNEY, is in honor of Jack McKinney, one of the pastors at this church whose Ash Wednesday sermon preparations served as the inspiration for the responsive worship song. It is effectively presented with cantor, congregation, piano, and chime tree, and can also be accompanied with guitar.

110.   Come and Feast, for All Are Welcomed

In 2004, this text by Larry Schultz was declared winner of a Communion Hymn Search conducted by Orange United Methodist Church, Chapel Hill, North Carolina. Liturgically, stanzas 1-3 serve as an effective Call to the Table, expressing a welcoming and inclusive invitation to all. Stanza 4 with the tune's descant functions as a vibrant expression to send the congregation forth from worship. Stanza 3 highlights the use of the five senses in the act of communion. A suggested worship use is to have a choir slowly and expressively sing stanza 3 while communion celebrants lift the cup and break the bread as the related text is sung; this allows the congregation to visualize the action.

113 (113a).   Arise, My Love

Larry Schultz wrote this hymn in celebration of his wife, Cindy, on the occasion of their 17th wedding anniversary. The text is a metrical setting of Song of Songs 2:10-13. He named his original tune CINDY'S SONG.

TOPICAL INDEX OF HYMNS

ADVENT

Midwife Divine Now Calls Us 92
O Come, Christ-Sophia 93
Sophia, Wisdom Deep in Our Souls 94

ADVERSITY

Are You Good and Are You Strong? 61
God like a Mother Hen 65
Hear our Prayer, O Christ-Sophia 71
How Long, Christ-Sophia? 13
Midwife Divine Now Calls Us 92
O Flower Blooming, Deep in Pain 90
Our Mother-Father God, We Praise Your Prophets Bold 6
Our Strong and Tender God We Praise 80
.... 80a
God Walks with Us 40
Through Distant Lands and Over Stormy Seas 23

ASSURANCE

Be Still and Know 56
O Great Creator, Loving Friend 7
Our Mother-Father Cares 63
Our Mother-Father God Is Near 38
Our Strong and Tender God We Praise 80
.... 80a

BEAUTY

Be Still and Know 56
Christ-Sophia Now We Bless 114
El Shaddai, O Holy One 46
God Like a Woman Long in Labor Cries 4
Hark! Wisdom's Urgent Cry 30

Midwife Divine Now Calls Us 92
O Come, Christ-Sophia 93
O Holy Darkness, Loving Womb 99
O Mother-Father God 74
O Mother Rock Who Bore Us 102
Sophia, Wisdom Deep in Our Souls 94
We Claim Your Support, Christ-Sophia, Our Rock 87
Welcome Our Sister-Brother Creator 19

CALLING

Come, All Who Long for Peace and Justice on the Earth 17
Awake to the Voice of Wisdom 28
Come, Holy Spirit, to Change Us 108
If This Is the Fast 101
Let All the Creation Sing Forth with Elation 79
O Holy Darkness, Loving Womb 99
O Sister-Brother Spirit 83
O Spirit of Power 18
.... 18a
Praise our God, Eternal Goodness 82
Rise and Speak Out 24

CALLS TO WORSHIP

Come, Father-Mother, Friend and Guide 31
Come Now, O Wisdom 2
Come, Thou from Whom All Blessings Flow 112
Creative Spirit, Come 54
O Brother-Sister Spirit, Come 8
O Holy Spirit, Mystery Within 41
Sister-Brother Spirit, Come 21

CELEBRATION (see also Praise)

A Living Celebration of Christ's Love 73
Arise, My Love 113
.... 113a
Celebrate a New Day Dawning 52
Christ-Sophia Lives Today 105
Let All the Creation Sing Forth with Elation 79
Loving Friend, Who Walks Beside Us 55
Praise Ruah, Spirit Who Gives Birth 76
We Sound a Call to Freedom 116

CHALLENGE

A Living Celebration of Christ's Love 73
Creative Spirit, Strong and Kind 29
How Long, Christ-Sophia? 13
If This Is the Fast 101
Let Justice Like Waters Roll Down 10
Like a Mother with Her Children 53
Loving Friend, Who Walks Beside Us 55
Midwife Divine Now Calls Us 92
Sister-Brother Spirit, Come 21
Rise and Speak Out 24
Rise Up, All People 5
Stir Us Out of Our Safe Nest, Mother Eagle 35
Wake Us All, O Christ-Sophia 16

CHRISTMAS

Christ-Sophia Now We Praise 96
Christ-Sophia Now We Welcome 95
O Christ-Sophia, Be Born in Us 97
Sound Forth the News That Wisdom Comes 98

COMFORT

Are You Good and Are You Strong? 61
Come to Me, All You with Heavy Hearts 70
Come, Weak and Weary Ones 60
God Like a Mother Comes Tenderly Near 62
God Like a Mother Hen 65
Like a Mother with Her Children 53
O Mother-Father of Us All 9
O Wisdom in Our Hearts 43
Our God Like a Mother Will Come 66
Our Mother Within Us 84
Our Strong and Tender God We Praise 80
.... 80a
Out of the Depths Christ-Sophia Is Calling 36
Share Our Grief, O Christ-Sophia 69
Tread Lightly on Your Heavy Path 37
With Arms of Comfort God Comes Near 67

COMMUNION

Celebrate a New Day Dawning 52
Come and Feast, for All Are Welcomed 110
We Invite All to Join our Circle Wide 111

COMMUNITY

A Living Celebration of Christ's Love 73
Celebrate a New Day Dawning 52
Come and Feast, for All Are Welcomed 110
Come, Holy Spirit, to Change Us 108
Come, Sister-Brother Spirit 45
Rise Up, All People 5
Sister Spirit, Brother Spirit 1
.... 1a
We Gather with Hope and a Vision of Peace 109
We Invite All to Join our Circle Wide 111
Welcome New Wineskins 57

COURAGE

Christ-Sophia Now We Praise 96
Christ-Sophia, Wise and Fair 39
Come, Thou from Whom All Blessings Flow 112
Hear our Prayer, O Christ-Sophia 71
O Christ-Sophia, Holy One 27
O Flower Blooming, Deep in Pain 90
Our Mother Within Us 84
Send Us Forth, O Christ-Sophia 86
Sophia, Wisdom Deep in Our Souls 94
Tread Lightly on Your Heavy Path 37

COVENANT

Arise, My Love 113
.... 113a
O Come, Join Hands, All Violence Cease 12
Our Mother-Father God, We Praise Your Prophets Bold 6
Rise Up, All People 5
We Give Thanks to You, Dear Earth 115

CREATION

Arise, My Love 113
.... 113a
Christ-Sophia Now We Bless 114
Christ-Sophia Now We Welcome 95
Gather Us Under Your Warm Wings 11
God Like a Woman Long in Labor Cries 4
Let All the Creation Sing Forth with Elation 79
Praise Ruah, Spirit Who Gives Birth 76
Sophia, Wisdom Deep in Our Souls 94

The Heavens Sing the Majesty of All That Ruah Made 78
Womb of All Creation Flowing 48

DIVERSITY (see Unity and Diversity)

DIVINE IMAGES

Advocate
    O Holy Spirit, Mystery Within 41
Bread of New Life
    Christ-Sophia, Well of Freedom 59
    Come, Father-Mother, Friend and Guide 31
    We Praise our God of Many Names 72
Brother-Sister Spirit
    Come, Father-Mother, Friend and Guide 31
    Join Now with New Power, Marching on for Peace 15
    O Brother-Sister Spirit, Come 8
Christ-Sophia
    Celebrate a New Day Dawning 52
    Christ-Sophia Lives Today 105
    Christ-Sophia Now We Bless 114
    Christ-Sophia Now We Praise 96
    Christ-Sophia Now We Welcome 95
    Christ-Sophia, Well of Freedom 59
    Christ-Sophia, Wise and Fair 39
    Come, Christ-Sophia, Healing Power 68
    Come, Christ-Sophia, Our Way 88
    Come, Holy Beauty 77
    Come to Me, All You with Heavy Hearts 70
    Do You Want to Be Healed? 103
    Friend and Source of All Creation 33
    Go Forth, O Christ-Sophia 91
    Hear our Prayer, O Christ-Sophia 71
    Holy Christ-Sophia 26
    Hope of Glory, Living in Us 85
    How Long, Christ-Sophia? 13
    Let Justice Like Waters Roll Down 10
    New Miracles Unfold 81
    O Blessed Christ-Sophia 104
    O Christ-Sophia, Be Born in Us 97
    O Christ-Sophia, Give us Power 34
    O Christ-Sophia, Holy One 27
    O Christ-Sophia, Rise 51
    O Come, Christ-Sophia 93
    O Come, Join Hands, All Violence Cease 12
    O Holy Darkness, Loving Womb 99
    Out of the Depths Christ-Sophia Is Calling 36

Rise Up, O Christ-Sophia 89
Rise Up, O People, Proclaim Christ-Sophia Has Risen 49
Send Us Forth, O Christ-Sophia 86
Share Our Grief, O Christ-Sophia 69
Tread Lightly on Your Heavy Path 37
Wake Us All, O Christ-Sophia 16
We Claim Your Support, Christ-Sophia, Our Rock 87
We Give Thanks to You, Dear Earth 115
We Invite All to Join our Circle Wide 111
We Praise our God of Many Names 72
We Sound a Call to Freedom 116

Comforting Guide
O Spirit of Power 18
.... 18a

Companion
Great Friend of All People 20

Creative Darkness
O Holy Darkness, Loving Womb 99

Creative Love
Listen, Now We Tell a Mystery 42

Creative Spirit
Creative Spirit, Come 54
Creative Spirit, Strong and Kind 29
O Christ-Sophia, Holy One 27
Praise Ruah, Spirit Who Gives Birth 76
The Heavens Sing the Majesty of All That Ruah Made 78

Creator
Come Now, O Wisdom 2
Creator God of Many Names 58
Holy Christ-Sophia 26
Love Rises Up 44
O Great Creator 75
O Great Creator, Loving Friend 7
O Spirit of Power 18
.... 18a
Rise Up, All People 5
We Praise our God of Many Names 72

El Shaddai
El Shaddai, O Holy One 46

Eternal Goodness
Praise Our God, Eternal Goodness 82

Everlasting One
Christ-Sophia Now We Praise 96

Faithful Friend
Father-Mother, Kind and Loving 47

Father
Creator God of Many Names 58

O Mother Rock Who Bore Us 102
Our God Is a Mother and a Father 22
We Praise our God of Many Names 72

Father-Mother
Creator God of Many Names 58
Come, Father-Mother, Friend and Guide 31
Father-Mother, Kind and Loving 47

Feast of Freedom
Christ-Sophia, Well of Freedom 59

Flower Sophia
O Flower Blooming, Deep in Pain 90

Fountain
O Holy Spirit, Mystery Within 41

Friend
Come, Father-Mother, Friend and Guide 31
Come Now, O Wisdom 2
Creator God of Many Names 58
Friend and Source of All Creation 33
God Like a Mother Hen 65
Great Friend of All People 20
Hear our Prayer, O Christ-Sophia 71
Love Rises Up 44
Loving Friend, Who Walks Beside Us 55
O Christ-Sophia, Holy One 27
O Great Creator 75
O Great Creator, Loving Friend 7
O Holy Darkness, Loving Womb 99
O Spirit of Power 18
.... 18a
Our God Is a Mother and a Father 22
Sophia, Wisdom Deep in Our Souls 94
Tread Lightly on Your Heavy Path 37
We Praise our God of Many Names 72

Giver of Life
Come, Father-Mother, Friend and Guide 31
Let All the Creation Sing Forth with Elation 79

Gracious Giver
Loving Friend, Who Walks Beside Us 55

Guide
Come, Father-Mother, Friend and Guide 31
Creator God of Many Names 58
God Like a Mother Hen 65
Love Rises Up 44
O Holy Spirit, Mystery Within 41
O Wisdom in Our Hearts 43
Tread Lightly on Your Heavy Path 37
We Praise our God of Many Names 72

157

Healing Power
Come, Christ-Sophia, Healing Power 68
Heavenly Dove
Come, Father-Mother, Friend and Guide 31
Come, Sister-Brother Spirit 45
We Praise our God of Many Names 72
Holy Beauty
Come, Holy Beauty 77
Holy Darkness
O Holy Darkness, Loving Womb 99
Womb of All Creation Flowing 48
Holy Night
O Holy Darkness, Loving Womb 99
Holy One
Come, Father-Mother, Friend and Guide 31
El Shaddai, O Holy One 46
O Christ-Sophia, Holy One 27
Sister-Brother Spirit, Come 21
Holy Spirit
Come, Father-Mother, Friend and Guide 31
Come, Holy Beauty 77
Come, Holy Spirit, to Change Us 108
Father-Mother, Kind and Loving 47
Go Forth, O Christ-Sophia 91
Holy Christ-Sophia 26
O Holy Spirit, Mystery Within 41
We Praise our God of Many Names 72
Hope of Glory
Hope of Glory, Living in Us 85
Light of the World
Come, Father-Mother, Friend and Guide 31
Life
Come, Christ-Sophia, Our Way 88
Lily
O Flower Blooming, Deep in Pain 90
Living Water
We Praise our God of Many Names 72
Love
Come, Father-Mother, Friend and Guide 31
Come, Weak and Weary Ones 60
Love Rises Up 44
O Spirit of Power 18
. . . . 18a
We Praise our God of Many Names 72
Loving Womb
O Holy Darkness, Loving Womb 99
Womb of All Creation Flowing 48

Maker
Praise Ruah, Spirit Who Gives Birth 76
Midwife
Come Now, O Wisdom 2
Midwife Divine Now Calls Us 92
Mother
Awake to the Voice of Wisdom 28
Creator God of Many Names 58
God Like a Mother Comes Tenderly Near 62
Like a Mother with Her Children 53
Our God Is a Mother and a Father 22
Our God Like a Mother Will Come 66
Our Mother Within Us 84
We Praise our God of Many Names 72
With Arms of Comfort God Comes Near 67
Mother Eagle
Stir Us Out of Our Safe Nest, Mother Eagle 35
Mother-Father
Come, Weak and Weary Ones 60
Our Mother-Father Cares 63
O Mother-Father God 74
Our Mother-Father God Is Near 38
Our Mother-Father God, We Praise Your Prophets Bold 6
O Mother-Father of Us All 9
Mother Hen
Gather Us Under Your Warm Wings 11
God Like a Mother Hen 65
Mother Rock
O Mother Rock Who Bore Us 102
Mystery
O Holy Spirit, Mystery Within 41
Power Divine
Come, Father-Mother, Friend and Guide 31
Redeemer
Holy Christ-Sophia 26
Loving Friend, Who Walks Beside Us 55
O Spirit of Power 18
.... 18a
Resurrection
Hope of Glory, Living in Us 85
Rock
O Mother Rock Who Bore Us 102
We Claim Your Support, Christ-Sophia, Our Rock 87
Rock of All Ages
Come, Father-Mother, Friend and Guide 31
Rock of Creation
We Claim Your Support, Christ-Sophia, Our Rock 87

Rock of Salvation
We Claim Your Support, Christ-Sophia, Our Rock 87
Rose of Sharon
O Flower Blooming, Deep in Pain 90
Ruah
Be Still and Know 56
Creator God of Many Names 58
Let All the Creation Sing Forth with Elation 79
Praise Ruah, Spirit Who Gives Birth 76
The Heavens Sing the Majesty of All That Ruah Made 78
Sister, Brother
Father-Mother, Kind and Loving 47
Great Friend of All People 20
Love Rises Up 44
O Christ-Sophia, Holy One 27
Our God Is a Mother and a Father 22
Sister-Brother Creator
Welcome Our Sister-Brother Creator 19
Sister-Brother-Friend
Love Rises Up 44
Sister-Brother Love
Celebrate a New Day Dawning 52
Come, Sisters, Brothers, Come 32
Sister-Brother Spirit
Come, Sister-Brother Spirit 45
Let Justice Roll Like Flowing Streams 3
O Sister-Brother Spirit 83
O Sister-Brother Spirit, Rise 64
Sister-Brother Spirit, Come 21
Sister Spirit, Brother Spirit 1
.... 1a
We Praise our God of Many Names 72
Sister Earth
Send Us Forth, O Christ-Sophia 86
Song of Freedom
Christ-Sophia, Well of Freedom 59
Sophia
Creator God of Many Names 58
Sophia, Wisdom Deep in Our Souls 94
Sophia-Christ
What Wondrous Thing 100
Sophia, Friend
Sophia, Wisdom Deep in Our Souls 94
Up From the Grave 106
Sophia, Wisdom
Up From the Grave 106

Source of All Creation
Friend and Source of All Creation 33
Spirit
A Living Celebration of Christ's Love 73
Christ-Sophia Now We Praise 96
Come and Feast, for All Are Welcomed 110
Come, Thou from Whom All Blessings Flow 112
Creator God of Many Names 58
Hope of Glory, Living in Us 85
Let All the Creation Sing Forth with Elation 79
Let Justice Like Waters Roll Down 10
Listen, Now We Tell a Mystery 42
O Come, Join Hands, All Violence Cease 12
O Flower Blooming, Deep in Pain 90
Through Distant Lands and Over Stormy Seas 23
We Gather with Hope and a Vision of Peace 109
We Sound a Call to Freedom 116
Spirit of Life
Be Still and Know 56
Spirit of Love
O Holy Spirit, Mystery Within 41
O Spirit of Power 18
. . . . 18a
Spirit of Peace
O Holy Spirit, Mystery Within 41
Spirit of Power
O Spirit of Power 18
. . . . 18a
Spirit of Truth
Be Still and Know 56
O Holy Spirit, Mystery Within 41
Thou From Whom All Blessings Flow
Come, Thou from Whom All Blessings Flow 112
Tree of Life
Hark! Wisdom's Urgent Cry 30
Truth
A Living Celebration of Christ's Love 73
Come, Christ-Sophia, Our Way 88
Way
Come, Christ-Sophia, Our Way 88
Well of Freedom
Christ-Sophia, Well of Freedom 59
Well of Love
Come, Weak and Weary Ones 60
Wisdom
Awake to the Voice of Wisdom 28
Christ-Sophia Now We Bless 114

Christ-Sophia Now We Praise 96
Come, All Who Long for Peace and Justice on the Earth 17
Come, Christ-Sophia, Our Way 88
Come Now, O Wisdom 2
Come, Thou from Whom All Blessings Flow 112
Friend and Source of All Creation 33
Great Wisdom, Queen of All 14
Hark! Wisdom's Urgent Cry 30
Holy Christ-Sophia 26
Love Rises Up 44
O Come, Join Hands, All Violence Cease 12
O Wisdom in Our Hearts 43
Praise our God, Eternal Goodness 82
Rise and Speak Out 24
Rise Up, All People 5
Rise Up, O Christ-Sophia 89
Sophia, Wisdom Deep in Our Souls 94
Sound Forth the News That Wisdom Comes 98
We Give Thanks to You, Dear Earth 115

Wise and Blessed One
O Blessed Christ-Sophia 104

Woman in Labor
God Like a Woman Long in Labor Cries 4

Womb of All Creation
Womb of All Creation Flowing 48

Word
O Holy Spirit, Mystery Within 41

DOUBT

Are You Good and Are You Strong? 61
Hear our Prayer, O Christ-Sophia 71
How Long, Christ-Sophia? 13
Our God Like a Mother Will Come 66

DOXOLOGY

Come, Thou from Whom All Blessings Flow 112

EARTH DAY

Celebrate a New Day Dawning 52
Christ-Sophia Now We Bless 114
Come, Holy Beauty 77
Love Rises Up 44
We Give Thanks to You, Dear Earth 115
Womb of All Creation Flowing 48

EASTER (see also Resurrection)

Christ-Sophia Lives Today 105
Love Rises Up 44
Rise Up, O People, Proclaim Christ-Sophia Has Risen 49
Up From the Grave 106

EPIPHANY

O Holy Darkness, Loving Womb 99
What Wondrous Thing 100

ETERNAL LIFE

Come Now, O Wisdom 2
Hope of Glory, Living in Us 85
Listen, Now We Tell a Mystery 42
O Great Creator 75
Our God Like a Mother Will Come 66
Our Strong and Tender God We Praise 80
.... 80a
With Arms of Comfort God Comes Near 67

FAITH AND TRUST

Gather Us Under Your Warm Wings 11
God Like a Mother Hen 65
Hope of Glory, Living in Us 85
Like a Mother with Her Children 53
Midwife Divine Now Calls Us 92
O Flower Blooming, Deep in Pain 90
O Holy Spirit, Mystery Within 41
O Wisdom in Our Hearts 43
Our God Like a Mother Will Come 66
Our Mother-Father God Is Near 38
Stir Us Out of Our Safe Nest, Mother Eagle 35
The Heavens Sing the Majesty of All That Ruah Made 78

FORGIVENESS

Come, Holy Beauty 77
Do You Want to Be Healed? 103
Gather Us Under Your Warm Wings 11
Hark! Wisdom's Urgent Cry 30
O Blessed Christ-Sophia 104
O Mother Rock Who Bore Us 102

FREEDOM (see also Liberation)

Celebrate a New Day Dawning 52
Christ-Sophia Now We Welcome 95
Christ-Sophia, Well of Freedom 59
Come, Sisters, Brothers, Come 32
Do You Want to Be Healed? 103
God Is She and He Together 25
God Like a Woman Long in Labor Cries 4
Great Friend of All People 20
Let All the Creation Sing Forth with Elation 79
Let Justice Roll Like Flowing Streams 3
Like a Mother with Her Children 53
Loving Friend, Who Walks Beside Us 55
O Christ-Sophia, Give us Power 34
O Holy Spirit, Come Dwell in Our Souls 107
Our God Is a Mother and a Father 22
Rise Up, All People 5
Sister-Brother Spirit, Come 21
Sister Spirit, Brother Spirit 1
.... 1a
Stir Us Out of Our Safe Nest, Mother Eagle 35
Tread Lightly on Your Heavy Path 37
Wake Us All, O Christ-Sophia 16
We Sound a Call to Freedom 116
Welcome Our Sister-Brother Creator 19
Welcome New Wineskins 57

GIVING AND RECEIVING (see also Stewardship)

Be Still and Know 56
Come and Feast, for All Are Welcomed 110
Come, Sisters, Brothers, Come 32
Sister Spirit, Brother Spirit 1
.... 1a
We Claim Your Support, Christ-Sophia, Our Rock 87

GRACE

Christ-Sophia Now We Praise 96
Christ-Sophia Now We Welcome 95
Christ-Sophia, Wise and Fair 39
Come Now, O Wisdom 2
Come, Sister-Brother Spirit 45
Creator God of Many Names 58
El Shaddai, O Holy One 46
Friend and Source of All Creation 33

God Is She and He Together 25
Hark! Wisdom's Urgent Cry 30
O Christ-Sophia, Rise 51
O Mother-Father God 74
O Mother-Father of Us All 9
Praise our God, Eternal Goodness 82
Share Our Grief, O Christ-Sophia 69
God Walks with Us 40
Sister-Brother Spirit, Come 21
Sophia, Wisdom Deep in Our Souls 94
Through Distant Lands and Over Stormy Seas 23
Wake Us All, O Christ-Sophia 16
With Arms of Comfort God Comes Near 67
Womb of All Creation Flowing 48

GRIEF

Come, Christ-Sophia, Healing Power 68
Come, Holy Beauty 77
God Like a Mother Comes Tenderly Near 62
Our God Like a Mother Will Come 66
Our Mother-Father Cares 63
Out of the Depths Christ-Sophia Is Calling 36
Share Our Grief, O Christ-Sophia 69
With Arms of Comfort God Comes Near 67

GUIDANCE AND CARE

God Like a Mother Comes Tenderly Near 62
Let All the Creation Sing Forth with Elation 79
Like a Mother with Her Children 53
Midwife Divine Now Calls Us 92
O Wisdom in Our Hearts 43
Our God Will Carry Us 50
Our Mother-Father Cares 63
Our Mother Within Us 84
God Walks with Us 40
Through Distant Lands and Over Stormy Seas 23
Wake Us All, O Christ-Sophia 16

HEALING

Come, Christ-Sophia, Healing Power 68
Come, Holy Beauty 77
Come, Father-Mother, Friend and Guide 31
Christ-Sophia, Well of Freedom 59
Creative Spirit, Strong and Kind 29

Do You Want to Be Healed? 103
Great Wisdom, Queen of All 14
Join Now with New Power, Marching on for Peace 15
O Sister-Brother Spirit, Rise 64
Sister-Brother Spirit, Come 21
The Heavens Sing the Majesty of All That Ruah Made 78
Wake Us All, O Christ-Sophia 16
We Invite All to Join our Circle Wide 111
Welcome Our Sister-Brother Creator 19
With Arms of Comfort God Comes Near 67

HOPE

Be Still and Know 56
Celebrate a New Day Dawning 52
Christ-Sophia Lives Today 105
Christ-Sophia Now We Praise 96
Christ-Sophia Now We Welcome 95
Christ-Sophia, Wise and Fair 39
Come to Me, All You with Heavy Hearts 70
Father-Mother, Kind and Loving 47
Friend and Source of All Creation 33
God Like a Mother Comes Tenderly Near 62
Hear our Prayer, O Christ-Sophia 71
Hope of Glory, Living in Us 85
Loving Friend, Who Walks Beside Us 55
O Brother-Sister Spirit, Come 8
O Christ-Sophia, Holy One 27
O Sister-Brother Spirit, Rise 64
O Wisdom in Our Hearts 43
Our God Like a Mother Will Come 66
Our God Will Carry Us 50
Our Mother-Father Cares 63
Our Mother-Father God, We Praise Your Prophets Bold 6
Praise Ruah, Spirit Who Gives Birth 76
God Walks with Us 40
Sister-Brother Spirit, Come 21
Share Our Grief, O Christ-Sophia 69
Through Distant Lands and Over Stormy Seas 23
What Wondrous Thing 100
Womb of All Creation Flowing 48

INCARNATION

Be Still and Know 56
Great Wisdom, Queen of All 14
O Wisdom in Our Hearts 43

O Holy Spirit, Mystery Within 41
O Spirit of Power 18
. . . . 18a
Share Our Grief, O Christ-Sophia 69

INDEPENDENCE DAY

We Sound a Call to Freedom 116

INVITATION

Come to Me, All You with Heavy Hearts 70
Do You Want to Be Healed? 103
Hark! Wisdom's Urgent Cry 30
Out of the Depths Christ-Sophia Is Calling 36

JOY

Arise My Love 113
. . . . 113a
Christ-Sophia Lives Today 105
Christ-Sophia Now We Bless 114
Christ-Sophia Now We Praise 96
Come, Christ-Sophia, Our Way 88
God Like a Woman Long in Labor Cries 4
Join Now with New Power, Marching on for Peace 15
Let All the Creation Sing Forth with Elation 79
O Brother-Sister Spirit, Come 8
O Christ-Sophia, Be Born in Us 97
O Come, Join Hands, All Violence Cease 12
Our Mother Within Us 84
Sound Forth the News That Wisdom Comes 98
We Sound a Call to Freedom 116

LABOR

Awake to the Voice of Wisdom 28
Come Now, O Wisdom 2
Come, Sister-Brother Spirit 45
Come to Me, All You with Heavy Hearts 70
Come, Weak and Weary Ones 60
God Like a Woman Long in Labor Cries 4
Holy Christ-Sophia 26
How Long, Christ-Sophia? 13
Midwife Divine Now Calls Us 92
O Come, Christ-Sophia 93
O Christ-Sophia, Be Born in Us 97

O Sister-Brother Spirit 83
O Wisdom in Our Hearts 43
God Walks with Us 40
Sister-Brother Spirit, Come 21
Sound Forth the News That Wisdom Comes 98
Welcome Our Sister-Brother Creator 19
Womb of All Creation Flowing 48

LENT

Come, Holy Beauty 77
Do You Want to Be Healed? 103
If This Is the Fast 101
Gather Us Under Your Warm Wings 11
O Mother Rock Who Bore Us 102

LIBERATION

Christ-Sophia Now We Praise 96
Creative Spirit, Come 54
Creative Spirit, Strong and Kind 29
Friend and Source of All Creation 33
Hark! Wisdom's Urgent Cry 30
If This Is the Fast 101
Let Justice Like Waters Roll Down 10
Listen, Now We Tell a Mystery 42
O Brother-Sister Spirit, Come 8
O Christ-Sophia, Rise 51
O Sister-Brother Spirit 83
Send Us Forth, O Christ-Sophia 86
Sound Forth the News That Wisdom Comes 98
The Heavens Sing the Majesty of All That Ruah Made 78
We Sound a Call to Freedom 116

LOVE

Arise, My Love 113
.... 113a
Christ-Sophia Now We Bless 114
Christ-Sophia Now We Welcome 95
Come, Christ-Sophia, Our Way 88
Come, Sister-Brother Spirit 45
El Shaddai, O Holy One 46
Friend and Source of All Creation 33
God Is She and He Together 25
Great Wisdom, Queen of All 14
How Long, Christ-Sophia? 13

Midwife Divine Now Calls Us 92
O Christ-Sophia, Give us Power 34
O Great Creator 75
O Mother-Father God 74
O Mother-Father of Us All 9
Our God Will Carry Us 50
Our Mother-Father Cares 63
Our Mother Within Us 84
Our Strong and Tender God We Praise 80
.... 80a
Sound Forth the News That Wisdom Comes 98
We Invite All to Join our Circle Wide 111

MINISTRY

A Living Celebration of Christ's Love 73
Creative Spirit, Strong and Kind 29
Friend and Source of All Creation 33
Go Forth, O Christ-Sophia 91
O Great Creator, Loving Friend 7
O Spirit of Power 18
.... 18a
Rise Up, All People 5
Rise Up, O Christ-Sophia 89
Send Us Forth, O Christ-Sophia 86
Sister Spirit, Brother Spirit 1
.... 1a

MIRACLE

God Is She and He Together 25
Hope of Glory, Living in Us 85
Listen, Now We Tell a Mystery 42
O Holy Darkness, Loving Womb 99
Midwife Divine Now Calls Us 92
New Miracles Unfold 81
The Heavens Sing the Majesty of All That Ruah Made 78
What Wondrous Thing 100

MISSION

A Living Celebration of Christ's Love 73
Come and Feast, for All Are Welcomed 110
Come, Sister-Brother Spirit 45
Friend and Source of All Creation 33
Go Forth, O Christ-Sophia 91
Great Friend of All People 20

If This Is the Fast 101
O Sister-Brother Spirit 83
Send Us Forth, O Christ-Sophia 86

NEW CREATION

Be Still and Know 56
Celebrate a New Day Dawning 52
Christ-Sophia, Well of Freedom 59
Creative Spirit, Come 54
Creator God of Many Names 58
Do You Want to Be Healed? 103
Let Justice Roll Like Flowing Streams 3
Like a Mother with Her Children 53
Love Rises Up 44
Loving Friend, Who Walks Beside Us 55
New Miracles Unfold 81
O Sister-Brother Spirit 83
Stir Us Out of Our Safe Nest, Mother Eagle 35
Welcome New Wineskins 57
Welcome Our Sister-Brother Creator 19
What Wondrous Thing 100

NEW LIFE

Christ-Sophia Now We Praise 96
Come, All Who Long for Peace and Justice on the Earth 17
Come Now, O Wisdom 2
Come, Sister-Brother Spirit 45
Come, Weak and Weary Ones 60
Do You Want to Be Healed? 103
El Shaddai, O Holy One 46
God Like a Woman Long in Labor Cries 4
Great Friend of All People 20
Hark! Wisdom's Urgent Cry 30
If This Is the Fast 101
Listen, Now We Tell a Mystery 42
Midwife Divine Now Calls Us 92
O Christ-Sophia, Be Born in Us 97
O Holy Spirit, Come Dwell in Our Souls 107
O Holy Spirit, Mystery Within 41
O Mother-Father God 74
O Sister-Brother Spirit, Rise 64
O Wisdom in Our Hearts 43
Our God Will Carry Us 50
Rise Up, O Christ-Sophia 89
Sister Spirit, Brother Spirit 1
.... 1a

Sophia, Wisdom Deep in Our Souls 94
Sound Forth the News That Wisdom Comes 98
We Give Thanks to You, Dear Earth 115
Up From the Grave 106

ORDINATION

Come, Thou from Whom All Blessings Flow 112
Send Us Forth, O Christ-Sophia 86

PALM SUNDAY

O Blessed Christ-Sophia 104

PARTNERSHIP

Celebrate a New Day Dawning 52
Christ-Sophia Now We Bless 114
Come, Sister-Brother Spirit 45
Great Friend of All People 20
Join Now with New Power, Marching on for Peace 15
Love Rises Up 44
O Christ-Sophia, Holy One 27
O Come, Join Hands, All Violence Cease 12
Our God Is a Mother and a Father 22
Our Mother-Father God, We Praise Your Prophets Bold 6
Rise Up, O Christ-Sophia 89
Rise Up, O People, Proclaim Christ-Sophia Has Risen 49
God Walks with Us 40
Sister Spirit, Brother Spirit 1
.... 1a
Wake Us All, O Christ-Sophia 16
Welcome New Wineskins 57

PEACE

Awake to the Voice of Wisdom 28
Be Still and Know 56
Christ-Sophia, Wise and Fair 39
Come, All Who Long for Peace and Justice on the Earth 17
Come Now, O Wisdom 2
Come, Sister-Brother Spirit 45
Creative Spirit, Come 54
Gather Us Under Your Warm Wings 11
Go Forth, O Christ-Sophia 91
God Is She and He Together 25
God Like a Woman Long in Labor Cries 4

Great Wisdom, Queen of All 14
Friend and Source of All Creation 33
Hark! Wisdom's Urgent Cry 30
Hear our Prayer, O Christ-Sophia 71
Join Now with New Power, Marching on for Peace 15
Loving Friend, Who Walks Beside Us 55
O Brother-Sister Spirit, Come 8
O Come, Christ-Sophia 93
O Come, Join Hands, All Violence Cease 12
O Sister-Brother Spirit, Rise 64
O Christ-Sophia, Give us Power 34
O Christ-Sophia, Rise 51
O Great Creator, Loving Friend 7
O Holy Spirit, Come Dwell in Our Souls 107
Our Mother-Father God Is Near 38
O Mother-Father of Us All 9
O Wisdom in Our Hearts 43
Our Mother-Father God, We Praise Your Prophets Bold 6
Rise and Speak Out 24
Rise Up, All People 5
Sister-Brother Spirit, Come 21
Sophia, Wisdom Deep in Our Souls 94
Sound Forth the News That Wisdom Comes 98
We Gather with Hope and a Vision of Peace 109
Welcome New Wineskins 57
We Praise our God of Many Names 72
Womb of All Creation Flowing 48

PENTECOST

Come, Holy Spirit, to Change Us 108
Creator God of Many Names 58
O Holy Spirit, Come Dwell in Our Souls 107
We Gather with Hope and a Vision of Peace 109

POWER

Christ-Sophia Now We Welcome 95
Christ-Sophia, Wise and Fair 39
Come, Father-Mother, Friend and Guide 31
Come, Holy Spirit, to Change Us 108
Come, Sisters, Brothers, Come 32
Creative Spirit, Come 54
El Shaddai, O Holy One 46
Father-Mother, Kind and Loving 47
Friend and Source of All Creation 33
Join Now with New Power, Marching on for Peace 15

Like a Mother with Her Children 53
Loving Friend, Who Walks Beside Us 55
O Christ-Sophia, Give us Power 34
O Great Creator, Loving Friend 7
O Holy Spirit, Come Dwell in Our Souls 107
O Sister-Brother Spirit, Rise 64
O Wisdom in Our Hearts 43
O Mother-Father of Us All 9
Our Mother Within Us 84
Out of the Depths Christ-Sophia Is Calling 36
Praise our God, Eternal Goodness 82
Sophia, Wisdom Deep in Our Souls 94
Through Distant Lands and Over Stormy Seas 23
Wake Us All, O Christ-Sophia 16
We Claim Your Support, Christ-Sophia, Our Rock 87
We Gather with Hope and a Vision of Peace 109
Womb of All Creation Flowing 48

PRAISE(See also Thanksgiving)

Christ-Sophia Now We Praise 96
New Miracles Unfold 81
O Great Creator 75
O Mother-Father God 74
Praise our God, Eternal Goodness 82
Praise Ruah, Spirit Who Gives Birth 76
The Heavens Sing the Majesty of All That Ruah Made 78
We Praise our God of Many Names 72

PRAYER

Come, Thou from Whom All Blessings Flow 112
Creative Spirit, Come 54
Creative Spirit, Strong and Kind 29
Great Friend of All People 20
Hear our Prayer, O Christ-Sophia 71
How Long, Christ-Sophia? 13
Loving Friend, Who Walks Beside Us 55
O Blessed Christ-Sophia 104
O Brother-Sister Spirit, Come 8
O Great Creator, Loving Friend 7
O Mother-Father of Us All 9
O Wisdom in Our Hearts 43
Stir Us Out of Our Safe Nest, Mother Eagle 35

RECONCILIATION

Come, Christ-Sophia, Our Way 88
Come, Holy Beauty 77
Come, Holy Spirit, to Change Us 108
Holy Christ-Sophia 26
O Come, Join Hands, All Violence Cease 12
O Mother-Father of Us All 9
O Mother Rock Who Bore Us 102
Send Us Forth, O Christ-Sophia 86

RENEWAL

Come, Holy Beauty 77
Come, Christ-Sophia, Healing Power 68
Do You Want to Be Healed? 103
Holy Christ-Sophia 26
Let Justice Like Waters Roll Down 10
O Mother Rock Who Bore Us 102
Out of the Depths Christ-Sophia Is Calling 36
Rise Up, O People, Proclaim Christ-Sophia Has Risen 49
Tread Lightly on Your Heavy Path 37

REPENTANCE(see Forgiveness)

RESURRECTION(see also Easter)

Christ-Sophia Lives Today 105
Listen, Now We Tell a Mystery 42
Love Rises Up 44
O Christ-Sophia, Rise 51
Rise Up, O Christ-Sophia 89
Rise Up, O People, Proclaim Christ-Sophia Has Risen 49

SOCIAL JUSTICE

Awake to the Voice of Wisdom 28
Christ-Sophia Now We Praise 96
Come, All Who Long for Peace and Justice on the Earth 17
Come Now, O Wisdom 2
God Is She and He Together 25
God Like a Mother Hen 65
God Like a Woman Long in Labor Cries 4
Go Forth, O Christ-Sophia 91
Great Wisdom, Queen of All 14
How Long, Christ-Sophia? 13
If This Is the Fast 101

Let Justice Like Waters Roll Down 10
Let Justice Roll Like Flowing Streams 3
O Brother-Sister Spirit, Come 8
O Great Creator, Loving Friend 7
O Holy Darkness, Loving Womb 99
Our Mother-Father God, We Praise Your Prophets Bold 6
Rise and Speak Out 24
Sister Spirit, Brother Spirit 1
       .... 1a
Sophia, Wisdom Deep in Our Souls 94
Wake Us All, O Christ-Sophia 16

STEWARDSHIP (see also Giving and Receiving; Creation)

God Is She and He Together 25
Like a Mother with Her Children 53
Loving Friend, Who Walks Beside Us 55
O Holy Spirit, Come Dwell in Our Souls 107
O Sister-Brother Spirit 83
We Give Thanks to You, Dear Earth 115

THANKSGIVING

Christ-Sophia Now We Bless 114
New Miracles Unfold 81
O Blessed Christ-Sophia 104
Praise Ruah, Spirit Who Gives Birth 76
We Give Thanks to You, Dear Earth 115

TRINITY

Come, Father-Mother, Friend and Guide 31
Father-Mother, Kind and Loving 47
Holy Christ-Sophia 26
We Praise Our God of Many Names 72

TRUTH

Christ-Sophia Lives Today 105
Christ-Sophia Now We Praise 96
Come, Christ-Sophia, Our Way 88
Come, Sister-Brother Spirit 45
Come to Me, All You with Heavy Hearts 70
Friend and Source of All Creation 33
O Christ-Sophia, Holy One 27
O Christ-Sophia, Rise 51
O Flower Blooming, Deep in Pain 90

O Holy Spirit, Come Dwell in Our Souls 107
O Wisdom in Our Hearts 43
Our Mother-Father God, We Praise Your Prophets Bold 6
Up From the Grave 106
Wake Us All, O Christ-Sophia 16
We Sound a Call to Freedom 116

UNITY AND DIVERSITY

Christ-Sophia Now We Praise 96
Come, Holy Beauty 77
O Holy Darkness, Loving Womb 99
Welcome Our Sister-Brother Creator 19

VISION

Be Still and Know 56
Celebrate a New Day Dawning 52
Christ-Sophia Lives Today 105
Christ-Sophia Now We Bless 114
Christ-Sophia, Wise and Fair 39
Come, All Who Long for Peace and Justice on the Earth 17
Come Now, O Wisdom 2
Come, Holy Spirit, to Change Us 108
Creative Spirit, Strong and Kind 29
Creator God of Many Names 58
Friend and Source of All Creation 33
God Is She and He Together 25
Great Friend of All People 20
Let Justice Like Waters Roll Down 10
Like a Mother with Her Children 53
O Holy Spirit, Come Dwell in Our Souls 107
O Mother-Father of Us All 9
O Spirit of Power 18
.... 18a
Rise Up, All People 5
Rise Up, O People, Proclaim Christ-Sophia Has Risen 49
Sister-Brother Spirit, Come 21
We Gather with Hope and a Vision of Peace 109
Welcome New Wineskins 57

VOCATION (see Calling)

WEDDINGS, UNIONS

Arise, My Love 113
.... 113a

WHOLENESS

Come, Christ-Sophia, Healing Power 68
Come, Christ-Sophia, Our Way 88
Come, Sisters, Brothers, Come 32
Come, Thou from Whom All Blessings Flow 112
Do You Want to Be Healed? 103
Friend and Source of All Creation 33
Great Friend of All People 20
O Blessed Christ-Sophia 104
O Christ-Sophia, Holy One 27
O Holy Spirit, Come Dwell in Our Souls 107
Our Strong and Tender God We Praise 80
.... 80a
Out of the Depths Christ-Sophia Is Calling 36
What Wondrous Thing 100
Womb of All Creation Flowing 48

INDEX OF SCRIPTURE REFERENCES

Genesis
1 . . . . 19, 76
1:1-2 . . . . 58, 79
1:26-27 . . . . 22, 77
1:27 31
49:25 . . . . 46, 48

Deuteronomy
32:18 . . . . 31, 102
32:11-12 35

Psalms
17: 8-9 65
19:1-6 . . . . 74, 78
22:9-10 92
23 . . . . 37, 40
30:5 69
36: 7 65
42 61
46:10 56
57: 1-10 63
65 79
74:3-7 13
89:5 81
92:1-5 82
94: 3-7 13
96:1 93
103: 13 22
104 114
104:30 56
131:2 67
138: 2-3, 7 . . . . 80, 80a
139: 7-18 23
139:9-18 75
139:12 99
143:8 55
144:9 84

150:6 79

Proverbs
1 . . . . 14, 30
1:20-23 . . . . 13, 17, 24, 106
1:20-25 28
2:10-11 43
3 . . . . 14, 30
3:13-15 89
3:13-17 . . . . 5, 12
3:17 112
3:13-18 . . . . 17, 24, 94
3:13-20 2
3:16-18 106
3:17-18 . . . . 70, 98
4 30
4:8-9 98
4:11 115
4:11-18 88
6:6-8 115
8 30
8:7-11 94
8:23-35 96
13:12 85

Song of Songs
1:5-7 90
2:1-2 90
2:10-13 . . . . 113, 113a

Isaiah
6:3 26
9:2-4 97
11:6 107
11:6-9 45
40:25 31
42:9,14 4

42:14. 43
43:1-2. . . . . 53, 66
44:2-4. 48
44:23. 79
45:3. 99
46:3-4. 50
49:15. 62
51:1. 87
53:3. 104
55:1-3. 59
55:8-9. 25
55:9. 58
55:12 . . . . 5, 12, 15, 52, 79
58:6-7. 15
58:6-8. . . . . 3, 101, 116
58:6-8, 11. 16
60:1-5. 49
61: 1. 8
66:13 . . . . 22, 31, 53, 62, 66, 67, 72, 84

Jeremiah
18:18-20. 6
31:22. 100

Hosea
11:3-4. . . . . 9, 50

Amos
5: 24 . . . . 3, 10

Micah
6:8. 7

Habakkuk
1: 1-4 13
2:2-3. . . . . 21, 105

Matthew
5:9. 15
5:9-12. 6
5:13. 86
6:25-30. 47
6:25-34. 38
9:17. 57
9:22. 49
11:28. 47

11:28-30. . . . . 60, 70
13:57 6
22: 37-40 73
23:37 . . . . 6, 11, 28, 65
25:35-40 86
26:6-13, 26-29 110
28:1-10. 105

Mark
1:10. 31
4:35-41 71

Luke
1:52-53 97
2:10-14 97
2:14. 60
4:18 . . . . 8, 10, 24, 26, 29, 33, 34, 64
11:49-51 28
13:20-21 86
19:42. 12
24:46-47 44

John
4:10. 72
5:2-9 103
6:35. . . . . 31, 72
8:12. 31
8:32 . . . . 41, 45, 51, 116
10:10. . . . . 36, 51, 59
12:12-16 104
14:6 . . . . 88, 89, 96, 105
14:15-17, 26-27 41
14:16-18, 26-27 21
15:12-15 . . . . 20, 33
15:15. . . . . 31, 72, 88
15:26. 31

Acts
2:1-20 . . . . 108, 109
2:17. 29
2:17-18 107

Romans
8:14-15, 26-27 83
8:18-25 85
8:19-23 . . . . 64, 77, 89

1 Corinthians

1:21-24 72
1:24 93
1:24-25 39
1:24,30 58
1:24-30 95
3:16 56
10:4 . . . . 31, 87
12:8-11 83
12:31 . . . . 1, 1a
15:51-54 42

2 Corinthians

1:3-4 67
1:3-5 . . . . 68, 69
5:17 . . . . 19, 81

Galatians

5:1, 13-14 32
5:22 8
6:15 55

Ephesians

2:14 12
2:14-15, 19 91

3:16-19 111
4:15 27

Colossians

1:27 . . . . 85, 95

2 Timothy

1:7 . . . . 18, 18a, 95

Hebrews

2:2-3 44
13:5 74

1 John

4:8 . . . . 18, 18a, 41
4:18 . . . . 18, 18a, 34, 41

Revelation

21:1-6 . . . . 1, 1a
21:4 . . . . 36, 69, 74
21:4-5 54
21:5 . . . . 17, 26, 58, 112

INDEX OF COMPOSERS, AUTHORS, AND SOURCES

African-American Spiritual, 70, 111
American Folk Song, 116
Atkinson, Frederick (1841-1897), 4
Bach, Johann Sebastian (1685-1750), 102
Beethoven, Ludwig van (1770-1827), 42, 52
Bennett, W. Sterndale (1816-1875), 49
Bliss, Philip P. (1838-1876), 28
Bourgeois, Louis (1510-1561), 112
Bradbury, William B. (1816-1868), 38, 40, 55
Converse, Charles C. (1832-1918), 71
Croft, William (1678-1727), 11
Crotch, William (1775-1847), 54
Cruger, Johann (1598-1662), 32
Cummings, William H. (1831-1915), 96
Darwall, John (1731-1789), 81
Doane, William H. (1832-1915), 46
Dutch Folk Song, 20
Dykes, John B. (1823-1876), 23, 26, 29
Elvey, George J. (1816-1893), 30, 114
English Carol, 94
English Melody, 100
Erneuerten Gesangbuch(1665), 49
Excell, Edwin O. (1851-1921), 68
Fillmore, James H. (1849-1936), 65
French Carol, 48
Gaelic Melody, 19
Geistliche Kirchengesang(1599), 92
Geistliche Kirchengesang(1623), 76
Genevan Psalter(1551), 54
Genuine Church Music(1832) (Joseph Funk), 87
Gesangbuch, Wittenberg (1784), 45
Giardini, Felice de (1716-1796), 88
Glaser, Carl G. (1784-1829), 80a
Gordon, Adonirum J. (1836-1895), 13
Goss, John(1800-1880), 82
Handel, George Frederick (1685-1759), 98
Hatton, John (c. 1710-1793), 44

Hassler, Hans Leo (1564-1612), 102
Hastings, Thomas (1784-1872), 39
Haydn, Franz Joseph (1732-1809), 16
Haydn, J. Michael (1737-1806), 18a
Hebrew Melody, 6
Helmore, Thomas (1811-1890), 12
Hemy, Henri F. (1818-1888), 75
Holden, Oliver (1765-1844), 34
Hudson, Ralph E. (1843-1901), 27
Hughes, John (1873-1932), 33
Husband, John J. (1760-1825), 109
Irish Melody, 2
Ivy, Karen (1950-), 76
Kirchengesang (1566) (Bohemian Brethren), 3
Knapp, Phoebe Palmer (1839-1908), 57
Kocher, Conrad (1786-1872), 35, 115
Kremser, Edward (1838-1914), 20
Lowry, Robert ((1826-1899), 17, 50, 53, 106
Lyon, Meyer(1751-1799), 6
Lyra Davidica(1708), 105
McGranahan, James (1840-1907), 108
Maker, Frederick C. (1844-1927), 9
Mann, Arthur H.(1850-1929), 83
Marsh, Simeon B. (1798-1875), 21
Martin, W. Stillman (1862-1935), 63
Mason, Lowell (1792-1872), 43, 62, 80a, 90, 98
Mendelssohn, Felix (1809-1847), 32, 96
Messiter, Arthur H. (1834-1916), 51
Miles, C. Austin (1868-1946), 66
Monk, William Henry (1823-1889), 35, 41, 115
Moore, William, 1a
Murray, James R. (1841-1905), 84
Peace, Albert L. (1844-1912), 67
Praetorius, Michael (1571-1621), 92
Prichard, Rowland H. (1811-1887), 85
Redner, Lewis H. (1831-1908), 99
Reynolds, William J. (1920-), 103

Sacred Harp, The (1844), 59
Sacred Melodies (1815) (William Gardiner), 8
Schlesische Volkslieder (1842), 77
Schultz, Larry E. (1965-), 1, 18, 22, 56, 58, 61, 73, 76, 80, 101, 110, 113, 113a
Schumann, Robert (1810-1856), 113a
Scott, Clara H. (1841-1897), 31
Shaker Tune, 22
Sheppard, Franklin L. (1852-1930), 74
Sherwin, William F. (1826-1888), 107
Sibelius, Jean (1865-1957), 56
Smart, Henry T. (1813-1879), 89, 95, 110
Smith, H. Percy (1825-1898), 7
Southern Harmony (1835) (William Walker), 37, 69, 103
Stainer, John (1840-1901), 100
Stockton, John H. (1813-1877), 64
Sullivan, Arthur S. (1842-1900), 15
Swedish Melody, 47

Tallis, Thomas (c. 1505-1585), 72
Teschner, Melchoir (1584-1635), 104
Thesaurus Musicus (1744), 14
Thompson, Will L. (1847-1909), 36
Tourjee, Lizzie S. (1858-1913), 25
Towner, Daniel B. (1850-1919), 24
Virginia Harmony (1831), 68
Wade, John Francis (c. 1710-1786), 93
Walton, James G. (1821-1905), 75
Ward, Samuel A. (1847-1903), 78
Warren, George W. (1828-1902), 5
Webb, George J. (1803-1887), 91
Webbe, Samuel (1740-1816), 60
Welsh Folk Melody, 10
Welsh Melody, 79
Willis, Richard Storrs (1819-1900), 97
Zundel, John (1815-1882), 86

ALPHABETICAL INDEX OF TUNES

ADESTE FIDELES, Irregular.. 93
ALDREDGE-CLANTON, 8.6.8.6.D.(CMD) 58
ALL THE WAY, 8.7.8.7.D. 53
AMERICA, 6.6.4.6.6.6.4. 14
ANGEL'S STORY, 7.6.7.6.D. 83
ANTIOCH, Irregular 98
ASH GROVE, 12.11.12.11.D. 79
ASSURANCE, Irregular 57
AUSTRIAN HYMN, 8.7.8.7.D. 16
AZMON, 8.6.8.6.(CM) 80a
BALM IN GILEAD, 7.6.7.6. with Refrain 70
BATTLE HYMN, Irregular 116
BEECHER, 8.7.8.7.D. 86
BETHANY, 6.4.6.4.6.6.6.4. 62
BLACK POINT CHURCH, 8.6.8.6.(CM) 80
BRADBURY, 8.7.8.7.D. 55
BREAD OF LIFE, 6.4.6.4.D. 107
BREAK BREAD, Irregular 111
BUNESSAN, 5.5.5.4.D. 19
CANONBURY, 8.8.8.8.(LM) 113a
CAROL, 8.6.8.6.D.(CMD)... 97
CHRIST AROSE, Irregular 106
CINDY'S SONG, 8.8.8.8.(LM) 113
CONSOLATOR, 11.10.11.10... 60
CONVERSE, 8.7.8.7.D. 71
CORONATION, 8.6.8.6.(CM).. 34
CRUSADERS' HYMN, Irregular 77
CWM RHONDDA, 8.7.8.7.8.7.7. 33
DARWALL, Irregular.. 81
DIADEMATA, 6.6.8.6.D.(SMD)..................................... 30
DIX, 7.7.7.7.7.7... 35, 115
DUKE STREET, 8.8.8.8.(LM) 44
EASTER HYMN, 7.7.7.7. with Alleluias............................ 105
ELLACOMBE, 7.6.7.6.D... 45
ES IST EIN ROS', Irregular 92
EVENTIDE, 10.10.10.10. 41
FINLANDIA, 10.10.10.10.10.10...................................... 56
FOUNDATION, 11.11.11.11.. 87
GARDEN, Irregular 66
GERMANY, 8.8.8.8.(LM) 8
GRACE STREET, Irregular.. 73
GOD CARES, 8.6.8.6.(CM) with Refrain........................... 63
GORDON, 11.11.11.11... 13
GREAT PHYSICIAN, 8.7.8.7. with Refrain.......................... 64

GREENSLEEVES, 8.7.8.7. with Refrain 100
HAMBURG, 8.8.8.8.(LM) 90
HE LEADETH ME, 8.8.8.8.(LM) with Refrain 40
HOLY MANNA, 8.7.8.7.D... 1a
HUDSON, 8.6.8.6.(CM) with Refrain 27
HYFRYDOL, 8.7.8.7.D... 85
HYMN TO JOY, 8.7.8.7.D. 42, 52
ITALIAN HYMN, 6.6.4.6.6.6.4. 88
J. MCKINNEY, Irregular 101
KREMSER, 12.11.12.12. 20
LANCASHIRE, 7.6.7.6.D... 89
LASST UNS ERFREUEN, Irregular.. 76
LAUDA ANIMA, 8.7.8.7.8.7.. 82
LEONI, Irregular... 6
LIGHT OF THE WORLD, 11.8.11.8. with Refrain 28
LOBE DEN HERREN, Irregular 49
LUX BENIGNA, 10.4.10.4.10.10.. 23
LYONS, 10.10.11.11.. 18a
MARCHING TO ZION, 6.6.8.8.6.6. with Refrain 17
MARION, 6.6.8.6.(SM) with Refrain 51
MARTYN, 7.7.7.7.D... 21
MARYTON, 8.8.8.8.(LM).. 7
MATERNA, 8.6.8.6.D.. 78
MELITA, 8.8.8.8.8.8... 29
MENDELSSOHN, 7.7.7.7.D. with Refrain 96
MIT FREUDEN ZART, 8.7.8.7.8.8.8.7.. 3
MORECAMBE, 10.10.10.10... 4
MUELLER , 11.11.11.11.. 84
NATIONAL HYMN, 10.10.10.10. 5
NEAR THE CROSS, 7.6.7.6. with Refrain................................... 46
NEED, Irregular... 50
NETTLETON, 8.7.8.7.D.. 59
NEW BRITAIN, 8.6.8.6.(CM) 68
NICAEA, Irregular 26
NUN DANKET, Irregular 32
OLD 100TH, 8.8.8.8.(LM) 112
OLD 134TH, 6.6.8.6.(SM) 54
OLIVET, Irregular 43
PASSION CHORALE, 7.6.7.6.D... 102
PICARDY, 8.7.8.7.8.7.. 48
PURER IN HEART, Irregular 65
REGENT SQUARE, 8.7.8.7.8.7. .... 95, 110
RESIGNATION, 8.6.8.6.D.(CMD) 37
REST (ELTON), Irregular 9
RESTORATION, 8.7.8.7. with Refrain..................................... 69
REVIVE US AGAIN, 11.11 with Refrain 109
SCOTT, Irregular.. 31

SHOWERS OF BLESSING, 8.7.8.7. with Refrain.................................. 108
SIMPLE GIFTS, Irregular... 22
SLANE, 10.10.10.10... 2
SOARING SONG, 10.10.11.11.. 18
SOLID ROCK, 8.8.8.8.(LM) with Refrain 38
SPIRIT DANCE, 8.7.8.7.D.. 1
ST. ANNE, 8.6.8.6.(CM).. 11
ST. CATHERINE, 8.8.8.8.8.8.. 75
ST. DENIO, 11.11.11.11... 10
ST. GEORGE'S WINDSOR, 7.7.7.7.D. 114
ST. GERTRUDE, 6.5.6.5.D. with Refrain 15
ST. LOUIS, Irregular 99
ST. MARGARET, Irregular... 67
ST. THEODULPH, Irregular.. 104
TALLIS' CANON, 8.8.8.8.(LM)... 72
TERRA PATRIS, 6.6.8.6.D... 74
THE FIRST NOWELL, Irregular 94
THEODICY, 7.7.7.7.. 61
THOMPSON, Irregular 36
TOPLADY, 7.7.7.7.7.7... 39
TRUST AND OBEY, Irregular.. 24
TRYGGARE KAN INGEN VARA, 8.8.8.8.(LM) 47
VENI EMMANUEL, 8.8.8.8.(LM) with Refrain 12
WEBB, 7.6.7.6.D.. 91
WELLESLEY, 8.7.8.7... 25
WONDROUS LOVE, Irregular 103

METRICAL INDEX OF TUNES

5.5.5.4.D.
BUNESSAN, 19

6.4.6.4.D.
BREAD OF LIFE, 107

6.4.6.4.6.6.6.4.
BETHANY, 62

6.5.6.5.D. with Refrain
ST. GERTRUDE, 15

6.6.4.6.6.6.4.
AMERICA, 14
ITALIAN HYMN, 88

6.6.8.6.(SM)
OLD 134TH , 54

6.6.8.6.(SM) with Refrain
MARION, 51

6.6.8.6.D.(SMD)
DIADEMATA, 30
TERRA PATRIS, 74

6.6.8.8.6.6. with Refrain
MARCHING TO ZION, 17

7.6.7.6. with Refrain
BALM IN GILEAD, 70
NEAR THE CROSS, 46

7.6.7.6.D.
ANGEL'S STORY, 83
ELLACOMBE, 45
LANCASHIRE, 89

PASSION CHORALE, 102
WEBB, 91

7.7.7.7.
THEODICY, 61

7.7.7.7. with Alleluias
EASTER HYMN, 105

7.7.7.7.D.
MARTYN, 21
ST. GEORGE'S WINDSOR, 114

7.7.7.7.D. with Refrain
MENDELSSOHN, 96

7.7.7.7.7.7.
DIX, 35, 115
TOPLADY, 39

8.6.8.6.(CM)
AZMON, 80a
BLACK POINT CHURCH, 80
CORONATION, 34
NEW BRITAIN, 68
ST. ANNE, 11

8.6.8.6.(CM) with Refrain
GOD CARES, 63
HUDSON, 27

8.6.8.6.D.(CMD)
ALDREDGE-CLANTON, 58
CAROL, 97
MATERNA, 78
RESIGNATION, 37

8.7.8.7.
WELLESLEY, 25

8.7.8.7. with Refrain
GREAT PHYSICIAN, 64
GREENSLEEVES, 100
RESTORATION, 69
SHOWERS OF BLESSING, 108

8.7.8.7.D.
ALL THE WAY, 53
AUSTRIAN HYMN, 16
BEECHER, 86
BRADBURY, 55
CONVERSE, 71
HOLY MANNA, 1a
HYFRYDOL, 85
HYMN TO JOY, 42, 52
NETTLETON, 59
SPIRIT DANCE, 1

8.7.8.7.8.7.
LAUDA ANIMA, 82
PICARDY, 48
REGENT SQUARE, 95, 110

8.7.8.7.8.7.7.
CWM RHONDDA, 33

8.7.8.7.8.8.7.
MIT FREUDEN ZART, 3

8.8.8.8.(LM)
CANONBURY, 113a
CINDY'S SONG, 113
DUKE STREET, 44
GERMANY, 8
HAMBURG, 90
MARYTON, 7
OLD 100TH, 112
TALLIS' CANON, 72
TRYGGARE KAN INGEN VARA, 47

8.8.8.8.(LM) with Refrain
HE LEADETH ME, 40
SOLID ROCK, 38
VENI EMMANUEL, 12

8.8.8.8.8.8.
MELITA, 29
ST. CATHERINE, 75

10.4.10.4.10.10.
LUX BENIGNA, 23

10.10.10.10.
EVENTIDE, 41
MORECAMBE, 4
NATIONAL HYMN, 5
SLANE, 2

10.10.10.10.10.10.
FINLANDIA, 56

10.10.11.11.
LYONS, 18a
SOARING SONG, 18

11.8.11.8. with Refrain
LIGHT OF THE WORLD, 28

11.10.11.10.
CONSOLATOR, 60

11.11. with Refrain
REVIVE US AGAIN, 109

11.11.11.11.
FOUNDATION, 87
GORDON, 13
MUELLER , 84
ST. DENIO, 10

12.11.12.11.D.
ASH GROVE, 79

12.11.12.12.
KREMSER, 20

Irregular
ADESTE FIDELES, 93
ANTIOCH, 98
ASSURANCE, 57
BATTLE HYMN, 116
BREAK BREAD, 111

CHRIST AROSE, 106
CRUSADERS' HYMN, 77
DARWALL, 81
ES IST EIN ROS', 92
GARDEN, 66
GRACE STREET, 73
J. MCKINNEY, 101
LASST UNS ERFREUEN, 76
LEONI, 6
LOBE DEN HERREN, 49
NEED, 50
NICAEA, 26
NUN DANKET, 32

OLIVET, 43
PURER IN HEART, 65
REST (ELTON), 9
SCOTT, 31
SIMPLE GIFTS, 22
ST. LOUIS, 99
ST. MARGARET, 67
ST. THEODULPH, 104
THE FIRST NOWELL, 94
THOMPSON, 36
TRUST AND OBEY, 24
WONDROUS LOVE, 103

FIRST LINES AND TITLES INDEX

Titles are in caps; first lines in lower case type.

A LIVING CELEBRATION OF CHRIST'S LOVE.................................... 73
Are you good and are you strong? 61
ARISE, MY LOVE.. 113
.... 113a
Arise, my love, my fair one, come... 113
.... 113a
AWAKE TO THE VOICE OF WISDOM 28
BE STILL AND KNOW... 56
Be still and know that Ruah dwells within 56
Buried and scoffed She lay, Wisdom, Sophia 106
CELEBRATE A NEW DAY DAWNING... 52
Celebrate a new day dawning, sunrise of a golden morn....................... 52
Christ-Sophia lives today 105
Christ-Sophia now we bless.. 114
Christ-Sophia now we praise 96
Christ-Sophia now we welcome.. 95
CHRIST-SOPHIA, WELL OF FREEDOM... 59
Christ-Sophia, Well of Freedom, may your springs of healing flow.......... 59
Christ-Sophia, wise and fair.. 39
Come, all who long for peace and justice on the earth 17
COME AND FEAST, FOR ALL ARE WELCOMED 110
Come and Feast, for all are welcomed at God's table spread with love...... 110
Come, Christ-Sophia, healing power 68
Come, Christ-Sophia our way... 88
Come, Father-Mother, Friend and Guide.. 31
COME, HOLY BEAUTY.. 77
Come, Holy Beauty, stir our full humanity 77
Come, Holy Spirit, to change us.. 108
Come, let us join our Sister Creator... 19
COME NOW, O WISDOM... 2
Come now, O Wisdom, we need your clear voice 2
COME, SISTERS, BROTHERS, COME 32
Come, sisters, brothers, come, and take the path to freedom 32
COME, SISTER-BROTHER SPIRIT 45
Come, Sister-Brother Spirit to make our world anew.......................... 45
Come, Thou from whom all blessings flow 112

COME TO ME, ALL YOU WITH HEAVY HEARTS 70
Come unto me, you weary ones 70
COME, WEAK AND WEARY ONES 60
Come, weak and weary ones, heavy with labor 60
Creative Spirit, come 54
Creative Spirit, strong and kind.. 29
Creator God of many names 58
DO YOU WANT TO BE HEALED? 103
"Do you want to be healed?" calls a voice tenderly...................... 103
El Shaddai, O Holy One 46
Father-Mother, kind and loving... 47
FRIEND AND SOURCE OF ALL CREATION................................ 33
Friend and Source of all creation, freedom flows forth from your love 33
Gather us under your warm wings 11
GO FORTH, O CHRIST-SOPHIA 91
Go forth, O Christ-Sophia, to make our world anew...................... 91
God is She and He together.. 25
God like a Mother comes tenderly near 62
GOD LIKE A MOTHER HEN.. 65
God like a Mother Hen comes to our side................................ 65
God like a woman long in labor cries 4
GOD WALKS WITH US 40
God walks with us to cheer and guide 40
GREAT FRIEND OF ALL PEOPLE 20
Great Friend of all people, strong Sister and Brother 20
Great Wisdom, Queen of all 14
Hark! Wisdom's urgent cry 30
Hear our prayer, O Christ-Sophia....................................... 71
HOLY CHRIST-SOPHIA 26
Holy Christ-Sophia, beautiful Creator 26
HOPE OF GLORY LIVING IN US... 85
Hope of Glory, living in us, Christ-Sophia, you we praise 85
HOW LONG, CHRIST-SOPHIA?.. 13
How long, Christ-Sophia, how long must we wait? 13
IF THIS IS THE FAST 101
If this is the fast we would choose 101
In faith we come together, Christ's Body in the world..................... 73
Join now with new power, marching on for peace......................... 15
Let all the creation sing forth with elation 79
LET JUSTICE LIKE WATERS ROLL DOWN................................ 10
Let justice like waters roll down on our land............................. 10
Let justice roll like flowing streams..................................... 3
LIKE A MOTHER WITH HER CHILDREN 53
Like a Mother with her children, you will comfort us each day............. 53
LISTEN, NOW WE TELL A MYSTERY 42
Listen, now we tell a mystery, told by prophets long before 42
Look, birds are flying in the air.. 38
LOVE RISES UP 44
Love rises up from deadly foes 44

LOVING FRIEND, WHO WALKS BESIDE US 55
Loving Friend, who walks beside us, giving strength for every day 55
MIDWIFE DIVINE NOW CALLS US 92
Midwife Divine now calls us forth from our safest place 92
New miracles unfold 81
O BLESSED CHRIST-SOPHIA 104
O Blessed Christ-Sophia, to you we lift our praise 104
O Brother-Sister Spirit, come 8
O CHRIST-SOPHIA, BE BORN IN US 97
O Christ-Sophia, be born in us, we need your power and grace 97
O Christ-Sophia, give us power 34
O Christ-Sophia, Holy One 27
O Christ-Sophia, rise 51
O COME, CHRIST-SOPHIA 93
O come, Christ-Sophia, full of grace and wisdom 93
O come join hands, all violence cease 12
O Flower blooming, deep in pain 90
O GREAT CREATOR 75
O Great Creator, Faithful Friend, loving us more than we can know 75
O Great Creator, Loving Friend 7
O HOLY DARKNESS, LOVING WOMB 99
O Holy Darkness, loving womb, who nurtures and creates 99
O Holy Spirit, come dwell in our souls 107
O Holy Spirit, Mystery within 41
O MOTHER-FATHER GOD 74
O Mother-Father God, your love surrounds us all 74
O Mother-Father of us all 9
O MOTHER ROCK WHO BORE US 102
O Mother Rock who bore us, unmindful we have been 102
O SISTER-BROTHER SPIRIT 83
O Sister-Brother Spirit, rise 64
O Sister-Brother Spirit, who dwells within us all 83
O SPIRIT OF POWER 18
. . . . 18a
O Spirit of Power, who dwells in us all 18
. . . . 18a
O Wisdom in our hearts 43
Our God is a Mother and a Father 22
Our God like a Mother will come 66
Our God will carry us 50
OUR MOTHER-FATHER CARES 63
OUR MOTHER-FATHER GOD IS NEAR 38
Our Mother-Father God, we praise your prophets bold 6
OUR MOTHER WITHIN US 84
Our Mother within us so holy and blessed 84
Our strong and tender God we praise 80
. . . . 80a
Out of the depths Christ-Sophia is calling 36
Praise our God, Eternal Goodness 82

Praise Ruah, Spirit who gives birth 76
RISE AND SPEAK OUT 24
RISE UP, ALL PEOPLE 5
Rise up, all people, let us work for peace 5
RISE UP, O CHRIST-SOPHIA 89
Rise up, O Christ-Sophia, for you the whole world longs 89
Rise up, O people, proclaim Christ-Sophia has risen 49
SEND US FORTH, O CHRIST-SOPHIA 86
Send us forth, O Christ-Sophia, on your mission in your name 86
Share our grief, O Christ-Sophia 69
Sister-Brother Spirit, come 21
SISTER SPIRIT, BROTHER SPIRIT 1
.... 1a
Sister Spirit moves around us; Brother Spirit joins in love 1
.... 1a
Sophia, Wisdom deep in our souls 94
Sound forth the news that Wisdom comes 98
STIR US OUT OF OUR SAFE NEST, MOTHER EAGLE 35
Stir us out of our safe nest; Mother Eagle come nearby 35
The heavens sing the majesty of all that Ruah made 78
The whole world was aching from violence and greed 28
THROUGH DISTANT LANDS AND OVER STORMY SEAS 23
Through distant lands and over stormy seas, keep us from harm 23
Tread lightly on your heavy path 37
UP FROM THE GRAVE 106
WAKE US ALL, O CHRIST-SOPHIA 16
Wake us all, O Christ-Sophia, by your liberating light 16
We claim your support, Christ-Sophia, our Rock 87
We gather with hope and a vision of peace 109
We give thanks to you, dear Earth 115
We invite all to join our circle wide 111
We praise our God of many names 72
WE SOUND A CALL TO FREEDOM 116
We sound a call to freedom that will heal our broken land 116
WELCOME NEW WINESKINS 57
Welcome New Wineskins, filled with new wine 57
WELCOME OUR SISTER-BROTHER CREATOR 19
WHAT WONDROUS THING 100
What wondrous thing is happening here 100
When all around the tempests blow 63
When we look all around 24
With arms of comfort God comes near 67
WOMB OF ALL CREATION FLOWING 48
Womb of all Creation flowing with your blessings everywhere 48

CPSIA information can be obtained
at www.ICGtesting.com
Printed in the USA
BVHW020415140223
658474BV00021B/273